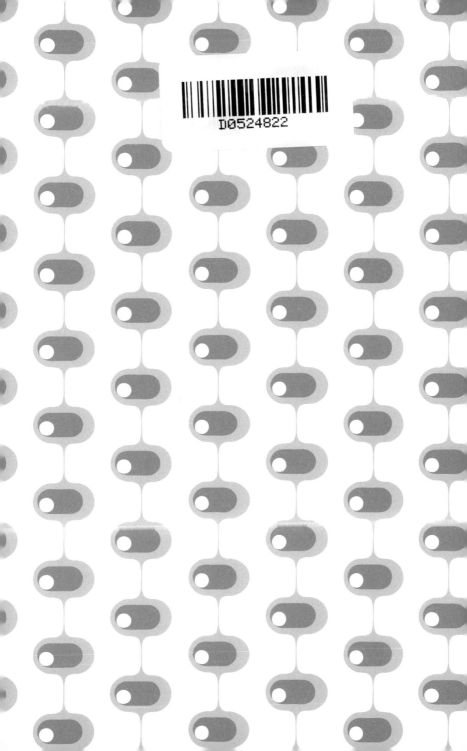

D0524822

CRAP
Dad Jokes

First published in the United Kingdom in 2013 by
Portico Books
10 Southcombe Street
London
W14 0RA

An imprint of Anova Books Company Ltd

ISBN 9781907554940

A CIP catalogue record for this book is available from the British Library.

10 9 8 7 6 5 4 3

Printed and bound by CPI Group (UK) Ltd, Croydon, CR0 4YY

This book can be ordered direct from the publisher at
www.anovabooks.com

CRAP
Dad Jokes

Ian Allen

PORTICO

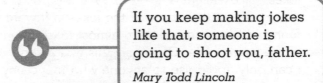

If you keep making jokes like that, someone is going to shoot you, father.

Mary Todd Lincoln

Hello again!

"In the whole of the New Testament
there is not one joke. That fact alone
would invalidate any book."

Friedrich Nietzsche

Thank you, Fred, for pointing out that, if God really is dead as you say, he certainly didn't die laughing.

When I compiled the first book of embarrassing Dad jokes (still excellent value at £9.99) it was pointed out by many readers that some of the jokes in it were far too funny, in fact some of them almost made them break into a weak smile. Obviously this was a serious error: I can only apologise to anyone who found any of the jokes in the previous book mildly amusing, and assure you that no stone has been left unturned to rectify the situation. In fact, I have gone to great lengths to find the most awful jokes possible for this follow-up.

If you do by some accident find yourself laughing at anything within these pages, please contact your doctor, as there must be something wrong with you.

Why, you may ask, does the world need another joke book, especially one full of terrible gags like these? Well, as someone once said, 'Even the longest jokes are better than the shortest wars.' And to prove it there are some longer jokes featured in these pages – and while I've had to tell them as briefly as possible, any Dad worth his salt should be able to spin out the signalman joke, for example, to a tale that would give the Anglo-Zanzibar War of 1896, which lasted just under 40 minutes, a run for its money.

And why are these Dad jokes so unremittingly awful? It's because Dads can't tell jokes – in fact they murder them – making it perfectly pointless to waste good material on them. So the world needs more bad Dad jokes to keep them away from the good ones. Ones like … erm … ah … I'm sure I'll think of a good one in a minute, I am a Dad, after all.

You see, there's only one thing worse than your Dad telling loads of useless jokes, and that's him telling the same few over and over and over again. For instance, when my daughter was little the only joke she could remember to repeat to us was:

Why did the banana go to the doctor?
Because he wasn't peeling very well.

We had to listen to that ruddy joke so many times that it actually spawned a brand-new joke all of its own:

What did the doctor say to the banana?
'Not you again?!'

This brings us to the important question: 'What is the ideal Dad joke?'

Well, as I remarked to my wife the other day, I now consider myself something of an expert on the subject. She readily agreed, while pointing out that 'ex' means 'has-been' and a 'spurt' is 'a drip under pressure'.

Be that as it may, I feel qualified to inform you that the classic Dad joke should have the potential to baffle your kids for years. Consider this one:

Q. What's the difference between a duck?
A. One of its legs is both the same.

Now, when they are very young, your kids may laugh just at the nonsense of this joke. When they are a bit older they may laugh because, though they still don't get it, they think they ought to and don't want to seem thick. When they are older still, they may laugh just out of sympathy for the decrepit old creature that told it. But by this time, hopefully, Pavlov's Law will have taken effect and you will only have to utter the words, 'What's the difference between a duck?' for them to roll around on the floor in hysterics.

They will hate you for it, naturally, but they won't be able to stop themselves and, in due course, if you've trained them correctly, they will repeat the procedure with their own children. And so the sadistic cycle will turn …

This book is proof, if proof were needed, that Dads just aren't as funny as they think they are. So, kids, grit your teeth and brace yourself for another onslaught.

And Dads, get ready for another battle in your constant war on humour, and embarrass your kids with pride.

Let the jokes commence!

Why did the man with a bad back go to Egypt?

To see his Cairo-practor.

How do you start a rice pudding race?

Say go.

A nervous expectant father tried to ring the maternity ward but hit the wrong speed-dial and got the cricket ground instead.

'How's it going?' he asked.

'Pretty well,' was the reply. 'We've got four out so far and the last one was a duck!'

Teacher: Jimmy, you've spent the whole lesson drawing a pair of stoats.

Jimmy: Sorry miss, I'm two-weaselly distracted.

First man: The chap trying to cross the Channel on a settee is now halfway across.

Second man: Yes, sofa so good.

Son: Dad, you've given me a pound short in my pocket money.

Dad: You didn't complain last week when I gave you a pound too much.

Son: Well, one mistake I can overlook, but not two weeks on the trot...

What's hairy and sneezes?

A coconut with a cold.

A concerned pensioner rang her 90-year-old husband while he was driving:

'Albert, be careful, they've just said on the radio there's someone driving the wrong way on the M6.'

'I'm on the M6 now,' he replied. 'But there's not just one going the wrong way – there's hundreds of them!'

32% of Dads admit to doing a household chore really badly so they don't get asked again (the other 68% are doing their best, they're just useless).

DAD STAT

Man: Can I have an asteroid pasty, please.
Butcher: What do you mean, an asteroid pasty?
Man: Well, like the one you sold me yesterday, only a little meteor.

What lives under a bridge, eats goats and sings?

The big bad troll-ol-ol.

What happened to the stupid Eskimo who lit a fire in his canoe to keep warm?
He discovered that you can't have your kayak and heat it.

What do you call a vampire with asthma?
Vlad the inhaler.

DAD STAT

The average age at which kids realise Dad just isn't funny is 5 years 11 months.

Here are the latest football scores:
Real Madrid 2, Surreal Madrid fish

Why did the sword-swallower swallow
an umbrella?
He wanted to put something away for a rainy day.

A conjuror was working on a cruise ship with his
pet parrot. All through his act the parrot would
squawk, 'It's up his sleeve!' or 'It's in his pocket!'
A fortnight into the voyage the ship hit a rock and
sank. In the morning all there was to be seen in the
vast ocean was the conjuror and his parrot, clinging
to a piece of wreckage.
After three hours the parrot looked at the
conjuror and said, 'Alright, I give up. What
have you done with the ship?'

Why did Little Miss Muffet get lost?

She curdn't find her whey home!

**What do you call
a vampire leading
a cub scout troop?**
Vlad the Arkela.

**How do you start
a cuddly toy race?**

Ready, teddy, go!

**Why wouldn't they let the architect build
a bungalow?**
There were too many floors in his design.

**Herbert and Horace were walking along a
country road when Herbert suddenly shouted,
'Crikey, they've buried someone by the side
of the road, and you ought to see how old he
was when he died – 175.'**
'If he was that old we'd have heard of him – what
was his name?' asked Horace.
'Miles, from London.'

What do you call a decomposing whale?

Mouldy Dick.

Did you hear about the contortionist who lost his job and fell on hard times?

He just couldn't make ends meet.

> **Teacher: Who was the Black Prince's father?**
>
> Tommy: Was it Old King Coal, miss.

Man: I've just been mugged by some bananas.

Policeman: Are you sure?

Man: Yes, there was a bunch of them.

Judge: You are charged with lewd behaviour, how do you plead?

Defendant: Not guilty. All I said to the conductress was, 'How much is it to Oldham?'

Patient: Doctor, I've just come out in spots, like cherries on a cake.

Doctor: Ah, you must have analogy.

Sergeant: I didn't see you in camouflage class this morning, Private.

Private: Thank you very much, Sarge.

Why didn't the man buy the duck egg?

In case it had a quack in it.

What athlete is warmest in the winter?

A long jumper.

Man: Could you tell me where the self-help section is, please?

Librarian: I could, but that would defeat the purpose.

Did you hear about the tourist in Spain who visited the Alhambra Palace 20 times?

He said it was very Moorish.

Why shouldn't you buy a chess set from a pawn shop? You'll only have half the pieces.

Why don't they eat custard in China?

Chopsticks.

Girl: If you had two cars, would you give me one of them?

Boy: Yes.

Girl: And if you had two houses, would you give me one of them?

Boy: Of course I would.

Girl: What about if you had two chocolate bars?

Boy: That's not fair – you know I've got two chocolate bars!

Who used to lurk in Sherwood Forest scaring pensioners?

Robin Hoodie.

Son: Dad, I don't like our goldfish.
Dad: Shut up and eat your dinner.

What do you call a man with no shins?
Tony.

First man: Can I use your lawnmower?
Second man: Help yourself, just don't take it out of my garden.

What happened to the butcher who backed into his bacon slicer?
He got a little behind in his work.

First bedbug: Are you pregnant?
Second bedbug: Yes, I'm having it in the spring.

Philosophy lecturer: Who can tell me where satisfaction comes from?
Student: A satisfactory?

What's the difference between a useless golfer and a useless skydiver?
The golfer goes WHACK! 'Oh no!' whereas with the skydiver it's vice versa.

Who is the coolest person in hospital?
The ultra-sound guy.

Why do farts smell?
So deaf people can enjoy them too.

And who's the coolest when he's away?
The hip replacement guy.

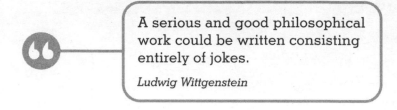

A serious and good philosophical work could be written consisting entirely of jokes.

Ludwig Wittgenstein

Rambler: Is it free to cross the field?

Farmer: No, the bull charges.

Patient: Doctor, I'm a self-obsessed kleptomaniac.

Doctor: Well, you'd better steel yourself.

Teacher: Where was Hadrian's Wall built?

Pupil: Around Hadrian's garden.

Herbert's phone rings in the middle of the night and he blearily answers it.

'Is that 385 3967?'

'No.'

'I must have misdialled, so sorry to have woken you.'

'That's OK, I had to get up to answer the phone.'

Son: Where've you been, Mum?

Mum: I've just been and got a radio for your dad.

Son: Sounds like a good swap to me.

Why did the Mexican push his sister off a cliff?

Tequila!

Teacher: Name a winter cereal.

Pupil: Readybrek.

Who led the Pedant's Revolt?

Which Tyler.

Dad: If you could choose to have a conversation with someone famous, living or dead, who would you pick?

Son: The living one.

Teacher: Why did Mary and Joseph find no room at the inn?
Pupil: Because it was Christmas.

Why can you only buy single eggs in France?

Because one egg is un oeuf!

Patient: Doctor, I think I'm allergic to rice.
Doctor: You must be basmatic.

Boy: Dad, I think I dreamed in colour last night.

Dad: No, son, it was just a pigment of your imagination.

Why did the clock scratch?

It had ticks.

A man was at the cinema and sat next to him was a boy with a dog. At the end of the film the dog started clapping.

'That's amazing,' said the man to the boy.

'It certainly is,' replied the boy. 'He hated the book.'

Dad: Put your coat on, I'm going out.

Mum: You don't normally take me with you.

Dad: I'm not – I've just turned the heating off.

Why don't you see penguins in Britain?

They're afraid of Wales.

What do you call a cat
with a bag of presents
in the desert?
Sandy Claws.

Which king was also
England's first chiropodist?
William the Corn-curer.

Teacher: Jimmy, are these your wellies in
the cloakroom?
Jimmy: No, miss, mine had snow on them.

What did the Smartie say to the chocolate button?
'For God's sake put some clothes on!'

Why did the chicken
cross the Möbius strip?
To get to the same side.

Dad: Ha! It says in the paper that men use 5,000 words every day and women use 10,000. I told you women talked more.

Mum: That's only because we have to repeat everything for men.

Dad: You what?

First man: I've just started dating a twin.

Second man: Do you have any trouble telling them apart?

First man: Well, it helps that her brother has a beard.

What has 100 legs and no teeth?

The front row of a Cliff Richard concert.

Why was the Egyptian boy confused?

Because his daddy was a mummy.

I was sitting in my lounge last night when –
Suddenly! – there was a tap on the door.
Say what you like about our plumber, but he's
a quick worker.

**Man: Have you found
my lost dog yet?**
Policeman: No, sir, we're
still looking for leads.

**Where did Noah
keep his bees?**

In the archives.

**My annoying neighbour was banging on my door
at three o'clock this morning.**
Luckily I was still up practising my drums.

**Son: Mum reckons someone's pinched a pair of
your Y-fronts off the washing line.**
Dad: The cheeky beggars.
**Son: She says she's not bothered about the pants
but she wouldn't mind getting the 20 pegs back.**

Horace got a job with BT knocking telegraph poles in. At the end of the day he went to get paid. The foreman said, 'I can only pay you ten pounds, all the other chaps have done ten times as many poles as you.'
'Yes,' said Horace, 'but you should see how much they've left sticking out of the ground!'

Son: Did you know the milkman was delivering to the newsagent yesterday and spilled the lot.
Dad: I hadn't heard anything.
Son: Well, it's all over the newspapers.

How can you tell a dyslexic Yorkshireman?

He's got a cat-flap on his head.

Herbert: I've just bought an amazing thing, a thermos flask – apparently it keeps hot things hot and cold things cold.
Horace: Sounds brilliant, what have you got in it?
Herbert: A cup of coffee and an ice lolly.

Two old ladies were in church listening to a long sermon.
One leaned over and whispered to the other, 'My bottom is going to sleep.'
'I know,' replied her friend, 'I've heard it snoring!'

Two idiots were walking down the road when a lorry went past loaded with turfs.
'That's what I'd do if I won the Lottery,' said one. 'Send my lawn away to be cut.'

What do you call a chicken in a shellsuit?

An egg.

> ### Herbert: I'm thinking of buying a Labrador.
>
> Horace: I wouldn't if I were you – have you seen how many of their owners go blind?

A old man in a large shopping centre walked up to an attractive young woman.

'Excuse me,' he said, 'I can't seem to find my wife.'

'I'm sorry,' said the woman, 'but I don't see how I can help you.'

'Oh, just keep talking to me,' said the man, 'and she'll turn up in no time.'

Japanese scientists have invented a camera with a shutter speed so fast it can almost photograph Chris Moyles with his mouth shut.

Dad: I've just received an email from someone who says he can read maps backwards.

Son: Dad, it's spam.

A man was passing a block of flats and saw a sign saying, 'Please ring bell for caretaker.' He rang it. After a couple of minutes an old chap opened the door and asked, 'What do you want?'
'Nothing,' said the man. 'I've just rung the bell for you.'

Doctor: We're going to put you in an isolation room and feed you pancakes and pizza.
Patient: Will that stuff cure me?
Doctor: No, but it's the only food we can slide under the door.

Two men were fishing by a bridge when a hearse and funeral procession went past. As it did so one of the men lowered his rod, took off his cap and stood in silence, head bowed.
'That was very respectful of you,' said the other fisherman.
'Well, we were married for over thirty years...'

First man: I've just been to my friend's funeral – he was hit on the head by a tennis ball.

Second man: That's terrible news.

First man: Yes, but it was a beautiful service.

Butcher: Can I interest you in eight legs of venison for £100?

Customer: No, that's too dear.

Do three dyslexics make a riot?

What's the difference between a financial adviser and someone reading this book?

One is all graphs and loans…

The average number of times a particular DIY job has to go wrong before Dad calls in a professional is 2.6.

DAD STAT

A man went to audition for a jazz band carrying two large bags full of mobiles – Samsung, Eriksson, all sorts.

'You don't appear to have an instrument with you,' said the band leader.

'No, but I've got two sacks of phones.'

A woman went into a hairdressers in Newcastle and said, 'Can I have a perm, please?'

'Of course you can, pet,' said the Geordie, clearing her throat. 'I wandered lonely as a cloud…'

> **What does Doctor Who eat with his pizza?**
>
> Dalek bread.

A man walked into a bookmaker's and asked, 'Can I back a horse in here?'

'Of course you can.'

'Righto, lads, back it in.'

A man was stopped by police at 2 a.m. and asked where he was going.

'I am going to a lecture about alcohol abuse, the financial ramifications it has on family members and the effects it has on the human body,' he said.

'Oh yes,' said the policeman. 'And who's giving that lecture at this time of night?'

'My wife.'

Son: Why is Mum cross with you, Dad?

Dad: Search me. She said she wanted something with diamonds for her birthday so I got her a pack of cards.

Nurse: There's a case of diphtheria arriving this morning.

Patient: Thank goodness, I'm getting fed up of Lucozade.

Teacher: What does acoustic mean?

Pupil: It's what a Scottish farmer uses on his cattle.

Teacher: Lucy, go to the map and find America.

Lucy: Here it is, miss.

Teacher: Good girl. Tommy, who discovered America?

Tommy: Lucy did, miss.

What do you get if you cross an ape with a set of drums?

A timpanzee.

A farmer buys a talking sheepdog and decides to test him.

'Go into that field and count the sheep,' he says.

The dog comes back twenty minutes later.

'Forty sheep,' he says.

'You're not so clever,' says the farmer. 'There are only thirty-eight.'

'I know that, but I'm a sheepdog so I rounded them up.'

A man was zipping along a country lane in his sports car when, approaching a tight corner, a car came round the bend. As they passed closely, the lady driver of the other car wound down her window and shouted, 'Pig!'

The man, incensed, started to make all sorts of rude and offensive gestures in the direction of the disappearing car.

Then he hit the pig.

I took my dog to the park today to play Frisbee with him.

He was useless – I need a flatter dog.

How much do seagulls get paid?

Nothing, they have to rely on tips.

Dad: Someone keeps pushing pieces of Plasticine through the letterbox.

Son: Yes, I don't know what to make of it.

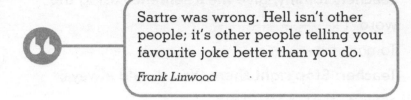

> Sartre was wrong. Hell isn't other people; it's other people telling your favourite joke better than you do.
>
> *Frank Linwood*

Herbert goes to the Antiques Roadshow:

Herbert: Look at what I've brought in – I've just found this great old metal box in my loft.

Expert: Are you insured?

Herbert: I think so.

Expert: That's a good job, because this is your water tank.

A man goes to the doctor and says, 'You've got to listen to my leg, it keeps talking to me.'

The doctor puts his ear by the man's thigh, and hears: 'Lend me twenty pounds.'

He moves down to the knee: 'I'm skint, just let me have a tenner.'

Finally he reaches the shin: 'Please, a fiver, anything.'

The doctor stands up and says, 'I know what's wrong with you – your leg's broke in three places.'

Teacher: Tommy, give me a sentence using the word 'I'.

Tommy: I is –

Teacher: Stop right there. You should always, always, always say, 'I am...'

Tommy: OK, miss. I am the ninth letter of the alphabet.

In what body of water is it important to know exactly where you are?

The Specific Ocean.

First farmer: Why have you painted white lines between those four rows of cabbages?

Second farmer: It's a dual cabbage-way.

What do you throw a drowning heavy-metal guitarist?

His amp.

A vicar was walking through the church's graveyard when he came across a man sitting on a bench.

'Morning,' he said.

'No, just having a rest,' replied the man.

What happened after the two jars of Marmite got married?

They had twiglets.

A ventriloquist at a club was making lots of jokes about how stupid footballers were, when a man stood up in the audience.

'I'll have you know that I'm a footballer and we're not all as thick as you keep making out.'

'I'm very sorry if I've offended you, sir,' said the ventriloquist.

'You keep out of it,' said the footballer, 'I'm talking to the little chap on your knee.'

Son: Mum's still mad at you, Dad. She says if anything happened to you she'd dance on your grave.

Dad: I know, son, that's why I've asked to be buried at sea.

What did Snow White sing while she was waiting for her photos to arrive in the post?

'Some day my prints will come...'

A man and his wife went to the pub.

'I love you,' he said.

'Is that you or the beer talking?' his wife asked.

'It's me talking to the beer...'

What do you call a professional footballer in a suit?

The defendant.

Two atoms left a restaurant, when one turned and said, 'I've got to go back, I've left an electron behind.'

'Are you sure?'

'Yes, I'm positive.'

Man: I've been robbed four times this month by the same man.

Policeman: Are you sure it was the same man?

Man: Well, he looked the same, but each time he was better dressed than before.

First man: I went to an open-air restaurant last week.

Second man: Was it any good?

First man: Well, it started raining just after I got there and it took me an hour to finish my soup.

First man: I come from a long military family – my grandfather fell at Waterloo.
Second man: That's impossible, he wouldn't have been old enough.
First man: A fat lot you know – someone pushed him off Platform 3 last week.

Judge: Will you please tell the court your name.
Witness: My name is Eric Stevenson, OBE, DSO, KCMG.
Judge: That's a funny way to spell Stevenson.

Why is a complex joke like a lift attendant?

It works on so many different levels.

Who do you send for if you want to know how many jars of rancid Italian sauce you've got in your fridge?
The Count of Manky Pesto!

Caller: Hello, operator, can you put me through to the king of the jungle, please.
Operator: I'm sorry, the lion is busy at the moment.

An overweight man went to see the doctor. The doctor said, 'I want you to eat regularly for two days, then skip a day, then eat regularly for two days, skip a day, then ring me in a fortnight.

A fortnight later the man rang the doctor. 'I've lost thirty pounds but it's nearly killed me.' **'Well, a lot of people find dieting hard,' said the doctor.** 'It's not the dieting, it's all that flippin' skipping!'

Harry Potter: Don't be so hard on yourself, you're not bad-looking.

Hermione: I didn't say I was bad-looking, I said I'm Muggle-ly.

Doctor: Put your tongue out please.

Patient: But I've come about my foot.

Doctor: I know, but I hate licking stamps.

Son: Mum says she's given you a choice – it's fishing or her.

Dad: Yes, I'm going to miss her.

> **King: Whoever marries my daughter will win a prize.**
>
> Prince: Can I see the prize first?

Dad: Johnny, go and wash your face, I can see the sauce from your breakfast this morning.

Johnny: That's where you're wrong, the sauce is from yesterday morning.

Judge: How do you plead?

Defendant: I don't recognise this court ... have you had it decorated?

> **What did the Frenchman say when he fell in the water?**
>
> Eau!

Doctor: Lie on the couch, please.

Patient: But I've only come about my wrist.

Doctor: Yes, but I'm trying to hoover the floor.

Patient: Doctor, I think I'm a kleptomaniac.

Doctor: Are you taking anything for it?

Patient: So far this week I've taken three TVs, two PlayStations and an X-Box.

Sherlock Holmes and Dr Watson were camping. Holmes woke Watson in the middle of the night and asked him: 'Look at the sky, Watson, and tell me what you can deduce.'

Always eager to impress his friend, Watson thought for a few moments then spoke: 'Well, Holmes, meteorologically the lack of clouds tells me it will be a fine day tomorrow; astronomically I see that the moon is on the wane and Mars is about to disappear below the horizon; astrologically I observe that Cancer is moving into conjunction with Scorpio; and finally, theologically, I can only wonder at the immense dimensions of the universe. What do you deduce, Holmes?'

'Watson, you idiot. Someone has stolen our tent!'

How do you tell the difference between tinned salmon and tinned custard?

Open the tin.

Did you hear about the man who went to university to do a sheep degree?
He graduated with a BAA.

What does Professor Dumbledore put on his hanky when he's got a cold?
Albus Oil!

What do you get when you cross a German composer with a bag of sugar?
A Schubert dip!

What's a gazelle's favourite fruit?

An antelope melon.

Where do grannies covered in jewellery go for
a night out?
Blingo!

Patient: Doctor, I'm
addicted to Twitter.
Doctor: I'm sorry, I
don't follow you.

What was the
name of Sancho
Panza's horse?

Donkey Hotey.

Teacher: How did you break your leg, Jimmy?
Jimmy: Standing on a mat, miss.
Teacher: You can't break your leg by standing
on a mat.
Jimmy: You can if it's at the top of a helter-skelter.

First boat-keeper: Come in, number 9, your time
is up!
Second boat-keeper: Hang on, we've only got eight
boats.
First boat-keeper: Number 6, are you in trouble?

Dad: Why are you throwing bread in the toilet?
Son: To feed the toilet duck.

Teacher: What makes you think this music was composed by Paganini?
Pupil: It says so at the bottom of the page.
Teacher: You idiot, that says 'Page Nine'.

What should you do if an idiot throws a hand grenade at you?
Pull out the pin and throw it back.

Patient: Doctor, I think I'm a lift.
Doctor: Nonsense, you're just coming down with something.

Why didn't the teddy bear want any pudding?

He was stuffed.

It was a busy night in the Tarmac pub. Double yellow lines were drinking with disabled bays, pelican zigzags chatting away with Give Way markings. All of a sudden the pub went quiet as a piece of tarmac with a white bike painted on it walked in.

'What's up?' whispered a cat's-eye to his friend.

'You don't want to mess with him,' came the reply. 'He's a cycle-path.'

First continental plate: There's just been a big earthquake.

Second continental plate: Well it wasn't my fault!

Bob was always late for work: no matter how many alarm clocks he set he always overslept. Then one day he woke up at 8.15 and – skipping breakfast, dressing frantically and dashing for the bus – he burst into the office at one minute to nine to be greeted by his boss:

'Hello, Bob. Where were you yesterday?'

First scientist: I've just managed to cross a homing pigeon with a Rottweiler with a pygmy.
Second scientist: I think that discovery will come back to bite you in the bum.

Teacher: Jimmy, what is reincarnation?
Jimmy: Is it where you die and come back as a tin of condensed milk?

When you choke a Smurf, what colour does it turn?

Son: Mum, is it true like Granny says that Dad's a hard man to ignore?
Mum: Yes, son, but it's worth the effort.

Boy: Mum, did you know the lady next door is sunbathing topless?
Mum: But there's a hole in our fence!
Boy: Don't worry, Dad said he'd look into it.

Boy: What's the difference between in-laws and outlaws, Dad?

Dad: Outlaws are wanted.

What's the difference between a misfortune and a calamity?

If George Osborne fell into the River Thames, that would be a misfortune. If someone pulled him out it would be a calamity.

Teacher: Every time I open my mouth, some idiot starts talking.

Bill and Bob were walking down the street when a mugger jumped out with a gun and demanded all their money.

As they emptied their pockets, Bill gave one note to Bob, saying: 'By the way, here's that tenner I owe you.'

Farmer Jones and Farmer Giles were leaning on a fence, and Farmer Jones was describing the symptoms of his sick cow.

'My cow were just like that,' said Farmer Giles, 'so I gave her two gallons of turpentine to drink.'

Next week they met again.

'I gave my cow two gallons of turpentine like you did and she dropped down stone dead,' complained Farmer Jones.

'Arrr,' said Farmer Giles, 'so did mine.'

Teacher: Bernie, where's your homework?

Bernie: It blew away in a strong gust of wind, miss.

Teacher: I see … and why are you late?

Bernie: I was waiting for a strong gust of wind.

DAD STAT

1 in 7 Dads confess to sneaking out of a school play to find out how the football is going.

A man went into a pub with a dog. 'I will bet anyone a hundred pounds that my dog can speak.' Another man took the bet and the whole pub sat in silence for two minutes – including the dog.

The man left the pub humiliated and shouted at the dog, 'Why didn't you talk?' 'Relax,' said the dog, 'think of the odds we'll get tomorrow night.'

Mum: Why aren't you out playing with Derek?

Son: Would you play with someone who cheats all the time?

Mum: No, I certainly would not.

Son: Neither would Derek.

Dad: I'm really fed up today – I think everyone hates me!

Mum: Don't be silly, dear. Everyone hasn't met you yet.

Boy: I just jumped out from behind the door at Dad and he said it scared him half to death.

Mum: Here's 50p, go and do it again.

Who said, 'Yo ho ho, and a bucket of spit'?
Long John Saliva.

Two old ladies were sitting in a café.
'The food here is terrible,' said the one.
'Yes, and such small portions,' agreed her friend.

Who decided to make dyslexia such a hard word to spell?
The same person who thought it would be fun to put an 's' in 'lisp'.

Jim: Why aren't you eating your animal biscuits?
Joe: It said on the box, do not eat if the seal is broken.

Where does a boxer keep his press cuttings?

In a scrapbook.

Customer: Waiter, how does your chef prepare the chickens?
Waiter: He just tells them straight out that they're going to die.

What do you call someone who cheats at the Highland Games?

The Lying Scotsman.

What do you call a train loaded with toffee?

A chew-chew train.

Why is an Indian guitarist who's lost his instrument like a useless centre-forward.

They've both missed a sitter.

Customer: I'd like a goldfish please.

Pet shop owner: Would you like an aquarium?

Customer: I don't care what star sign it is.

What do you get if you cross a KFC with a female wizard with the Sahara Desert?

A chicken sand-witch.

Two boys watched a horse go past and leave a deposit on the road. One boy nipped out with a bucket and shovel and collected the dung.

'What are you doing that for?' asked his friend.

'My dad puts it on his rhubarb.'

'Oh, we have custard on ours.'

Teacher: Today we'll be looking at the alphabet and I'll be asking everyone what their favourite letter is.

Pupil: Please miss, my favourite letter is 'G'.

Teacher: And why is that, Angus?

Why was the calendar scared?

Because it knew its days were numbered.

I could easily tell that the solicitor had a will in his pocket.

It was a dead giveaway.

DIGITAL DAD

Dad's Text Shorthand

LOL	LOTS OF LOVE
LMAO	LEAVE ME ALONE OIK!
ROFL	REALLY OLD FORGETFUL LAYABOUT
BTW	BRING THE WHEELCHAIR
ILY	I'M LOST, YOU?
FWIW	FOUND WATCH IN WASHING-MACHINE
OMG	ON MY GUARD
IMHO	I MUST HAVE OVERSLEPT
MILF	MUM IS LOOKING FUNNY
KWIM	KIDS WILL (INEVITABLY) MOAN
KC	KICKED CAT
PITA	PLEASE INFORM THE AA
YOLO	YOU ONLY LIE-IN ONCE
RBTL	READ BETTER (IN) THE LIGHT
WYWH	WISH YOU WEREN'T HERE
SH	SHOPPING HAPPENS

Dad: Do you want to come to those new shops with us?

Son: No, once you've seen one shopping centre you've seen a mall.

First man: In the pub last night I just couldn't help breaking into a song.

Second man: I wasn't surprised, you obviously couldn't find the right key.

> **How do you mend a cracked parrot?**
>
> With polly-filler.

A man was at work one cold winter morning when he received a text from his wife.

'Windows frozen, in hurry, what should I do?'

He texted back, 'Pour hot water over'

Five minutes later he had another text.

'Tried hot water – now computer not working at all.'

> **What happened when the depressed man bought himself a scooter?**
>
> He moped around all day.

First man: Someone has just jumped off a Paris bridge into the river.

Second man: He must be in Seine.

Boy: Mum, would you say Dad has a well-balanced personality?

Mum: Yes, he's got a chip on each shoulder.

My window-cleaner's ladder has just got married.

He's pretty pleased because now he's got a step-ladder as well.

DAD STAT

Parents spend about 500 hours changing each of their child's nappies. Of this, Mums spend 450 hours and Dads 50, thus proving that Dads are more efficient than Mums...

Did you hear about the man who was sacked for gross incompetence and took his boss to an industrial tribunal?
He won his case, as he said he'd only been incompetent 143 times.

Why did the computer tech's toaster stop working?

He'd disabled pop-ups.

What do you call it when a lorry-load of apostrophes drives off a cliff?
A catastrophe.

Doctor: I want you to take this three times a day with water.
Student: What is it?
Doctor: Soap.

Where do farmers buy their cows?
From a cattle-ogue.

Son: Why do you say marriage is like a pack of cards, Mum?
Mum: Well, at the start, all you need is a diamond and a pair of hearts … after a few years you just want a club and a spade.

Son: What do you think about Mum learning to drive?
Dad: Well, I certainly won't stand in her way.

> **Son: Do you know where the yeast extract is, Pa?**
>
> Dad: No, but Ma might.

Mum: Go down the shop, son, get a bottle of milk, and if they've got eggs, get six.

Fifteen minutes later…

Mum: Why on earth have you bought six bottles of milk?

Son: They had eggs.

Sammy the shark was swimming in the sea when he saw his friend Wally the whale coming towards him. Wally had in his mouth the most unhealthy, disease-ridden octopus Sammy had ever seen.

With a flick of his jaws, Wally tossed the octopus in the shark's direction, saying, 'There you go, Sammy, here's the sick squid I owe you.'

How does a rabbit get dry after a storm?
He borrows a hare dryer.

Mum: You should go to see the doctor, you're addicted to drinking brake fluid.
Dad: No I'm not, I can stop any time I want to.

How do birds of prey look forward to Christmas?
Eagle-ly.

Son: Why are you putting a new battery in the clock, Dad?
Dad: Well, it was running slow, and last night it fell off the wall, and if it had happened a minute earlier it would have hit your Gran.

What's the difference between Dad's car and a golf ball?
You can drive a golf ball 250 yards.

Horace: I'm qoinq to have to get a new car. It can only get up to 75 on a hill.
Herbert: That doesn't sound so bad.
Horace: Yes, but I live at number 95.

An animal-loving Dad went up to a man in the park with a friendly-looking dog beside him.
'Does your dog bite?' asked Dad.
'No,' said the man.
Dad bent down to pat the dog, who suddenly snarled and gave him a nip on the hand.
'I thought you said your dog didn't bite?' asked Dad.
'That's not my dog,' replied the man.

What's the difference between a Dad and a shopping trolley?
A shopping trolley has a mind of its own.

If tin whistles are made out of tin, what are fog horns made of?

French knock-knock joke:
Frappe, frappe.
Qui est la?
L'ost.
L'ost qui?
Oui.

What was born to succeed?

A parrot with no beak.

Two cows were in a field.
'Moo!' said one.
'That's just what I was going to say,'
said the other.

Patient: Doctor, it really hurts my back when
I touch my toes.
Doctor: Well, stop doing it then.

What do you call a teacher with no arms, no legs and no body?

The head.

Two owls were playing pool. The first owl was bending over a shot when his wing hit another ball.

'That's two hits,' said his friend.

'Two hits to who?' asked the first owl.

Customer: Can I have a wasp, please?

Baker: Don't be daft, we don't sell wasps.

Customer: But you've got some in the window.

A white horse goes into a pub and asks for a beer.

'That's funny,' says the barman, 'we've got a whisky named after you.'

'What,' says the horse, 'Roger?'

Who'd win in a fight, an extra-strong mint or a Hall's?

The Hall's – he's completely menthol.

Why does a chicken coop have two doors?

If it had four doors it would be a chicken sedan.

A man went to the pub and ordered a pint of beer. As he sat drinking, he heard little voices saying, 'That's a nice jacket,' and 'Those glasses really suit you.'

The barman saw him looking puzzled and said, 'Don't worry, sir, the peanuts are complimentary.'

Did you hear about the stupid farmer who wanted to produce lean beef?
He cut the left-hand legs off all his cows.

Son: Mum, why does God use our bathroom?
Mum: What makes you think God uses our bathroom?
Son: Well, every morning I see Dad standing outside saying, 'God, how much longer are you going to be in there?'

What do you call an aardvark that cries at sad films?
A vark.

What has two legs and bleeds?
Half a cat.

Did you hear about the idiot who stayed up all night wondering where the sun had gone?
It finally dawned on him.

First magician: Who was that lady I sawed you with last night?
Second magician: That was no lady, that was my half-sister.

Why don't the England cricket team get vaccinations before going on tour?
Because they never catch anything.

Why did the ram run over the cliff?

He didn't see the ewe turn.

A policeman sees a drunk on his hands and knees under a street light and asks him what he's doing.
'I'm looking for my keys.'
The policeman decides to help him but after five minutes they've found nothing and he asks, 'Are you sure this is where you dropped them?'
'Oh no,' says the drunk, 'I dropped them down the road but the light's much better here.'

First penguin: Ha, ha, you look like you're wearing a tuxedo.

Second penguin (enigmatically): Who says I'm not?

What happened in the boxing match between the hedgehog and the mole?

The hedgehog won on points.

What's grey and goes bang, bang, bang, bang?

A four-door elephant.

> **What's brown, grows on trees and can't sing?**
>
> Des O'Conker.

At the International Farmers' Convention a Texan was bragging to his British counterpart.

'I can get in my car in a morning, drive all day and still be on my own farm.'

'Arr,' said the Brit, 'I had a car like that once.'

A vicar went to a pet shop to buy a parrot. 'This one will be just right for you,' said the assistant. 'It has a string on each leg, and if you pull the string on the right leg he recites the Lord's Prayer, and if you pull the string on the left leg he sings a hymn.'

'Wonderful,' said the vicar. 'And what happens if I pull them both at once?'

'I fall off my flippin' perch, you pillock,' said the parrot.

What's black and shiny and swashbuckling?

Binbag the Sailor.

What's black and white and eats like a horse?

A zebra.

Which is braver, a stone or a rock?

A rock, because it's a little boulder.

Teacher: Name two crustaceans?

Pupil: Err, Kings Crustacean and Charing Crustacean.

Boy in museum: How old is that stegosaurus skeleton?

Curator: It is 150 million years and six months old.

Boy: How can you be so accurate?

Curator: When I started here someone told me it was 150 million years old, and I've been here for six months.

What's red and sits in the corner?

A naughty pillar box.

A hunter was walking through the woods when a beautiful women wearing hardly any clothes stepped from behind a tree.

'Crikey, are you game?' he asked.

'Yes,' she replied.

So he shot her.

Boy: I'd like to buy a mouth organ please.

Shopkeeper: That's funny, I don't sell many but I had a girl in here only yesterday asking for the same thing.

Boy: That must have been our Monica.

Why is one side of a 'V' of geese always longer?

Because there are more geese on that side.

First man: You look worried.

Second man: I am. The doctor's just told me I'll have to take a certain tablet every day for the rest of my life.

First man: Well, that's not so bad.

Second man: Yes, but he's only given me a prescription for a month!

What's the most musical fish?

A piano tuna.

Teacher: Give me a sentence using the word 'pregnant'.

Timmy: The fireman came down the ladder pregnant.

Teacher: I don't think you know what 'pregnant' means.

Timmy: Yes I do, it means 'carrying a child'.

What's the difference between a tennis ball and the Prince of Wales?

One is thrown to the air and the other is heir to the throne.

Horace and Herbert were driving a big van down a country lane when they came to a bridge marked, 'Maximum height – 10ft 6in'.

They stopped the van and measured its height – it was 12ft tall.

Herbert looked up and down the road and said, 'There's no police in sight – I say we risk it.'

Why do divers fall out of the boat backwards to get into the water?
Because if they jumped forward they'd still be in the boat.

What happens if you don't pay your exorcist?
You get repossessed.

> **A square and a circle go into a pub.**
>
> The square said, 'Your round.'

Receptionist: Doctor, there's a man here who says he thinks he's invisible.
Doctor: Tell him I can't see him.

Patient: I keep seeing spots before my eyes.
Doctor: Have you seen an optician?
Patient: No, just spots.

A man got on to the train platform just as the doors were closing. He started to run but the train began to pull away and although he chased it for a few seconds he ended up puffing and blowing, watching it disappear into the distance.

An old man came up to him and said, rather obviously, 'Miss the train?'

'Not really,' panted the man, 'I never got to know it very well.'

Charles Dickens went into a cocktail bar and ordered a Martini.

The barman said, 'Olive or twist?'

What do you give dead bread?

A toast mortem.

First farmer: Do your cows smoke?
Second farmer: No.
First farmer: In that case your barn is on fire.

A monastery falls on hard times so decides to open a fish and chip shop. At the grand opening, the first customer comes up to the man in a habit behind the counter and says, 'I suppose you're the fish friar!'

'No,' replies the man, 'I'm the chip monk!'

Judge: Why do want to change your plea to guilty now? You have wasted the court's time.

Defendant: I'm sorry, your honour, but now I've heard all the evidence against me I realise I must have done it.

Patient: Doctor, I've just swallowed a camera.

Doctor: Well, come back next week and we'll see what develops.

Herbert: I think the Miss Universe contest is fixed.

Horace: Why do you say that?

Herbert: Because the winner is always from Earth.

A man looked over his fence and saw the neighbour's little boy digging a hole.

'What are you digging that hole for, Johnny?'

'I'm burying my pet mouse.'

'That's a big hole for a mouse.'

'Well, he's inside your cat.'

What should you do if your mouth ices up?

Grit your teeth

Two ostriches fall out and the big one starts chasing the small one. Just as he's about to catch him, the little ostrich sticks his head in the sand. 'That's strange,' says the big ostrich, coming to a halt. 'Where did he go?'

What's green and always points north?

A magnetic cucumber.

Why is six o'clock in the morning like a pig's tail?

Because it's twirly.

A pair of shipwrecked sailors were adrift in a lifeboat. They had a packet of cigarettes but no matches. How did they manage?

They threw one cigarette out of the boat and then it was a cigarette lighter!

A man went into a pub with a giraffe. They had six pints of bitter each, after which the giraffe collapsed in a heap. The man looked down at it and went to leave.

The barman shouted, 'Oi, you can't leave that lying down there.'

'It's not a lion,' replied the man, 'it's a giraffe.'

What's the difference between a coyote and a flea?

One howls on the prairie and the other prowls on the hairy.

What's yellow and can't ski?

A bulldozer.

Bad news. A ship carrying artificial limbs has sunk with the loss of all hands.

Why do squirrels swim on their backs?

To keep their nuts dry.

Did you hear about the stupid dog lying by the fire, eating a bone?

When it got up it only had three legs.

A woman went to the police station to report her husband missing. When asked to describe him, she said he was 'about 25, six feet tall, slim and muscular with black wavy hair'.

'Hang on,' said the policeman, 'I think I know your husband – he's fat, forty and bald.'

'Exactly,' said the woman, 'but who wants him back?'

Dad: Are you still going to that origami club at school?

Son: No, it folded.

What's red and smells like blue paint?

Red paint.

**Brutus loved chocolate biscuits, and put six on
a plate for when his friend Julius Caesar came to
tea. Brutus nipped off to the toilet and when he
came back, the biscuits and Caesar were gone.**
He dashed after Caesar, caught him at the Forum,
whipped out his knife and stabbed him.
**Caesar looked at the knife, looked at his old
friend and said, 'Et tu, Brutus?'**
'You liar,' said Brutus, 'you had all six!'

**Mum: Why are you so
late home?**
Dad: There was a power
cut at the Tube station
and I was stuck on the
escalator for two hours.

Mum: Where shall we go on holiday next year?

Dad: I'd like to go somewhere I've never been before.

Mum: How about the kitchen?

Daughter: Mum, who's cleverer, men or women?

Mum: Well, diamonds are a girl's best friend, and man's best friend is a dog – you work it out.

Dad: Be honest, do you ever look at a man and wish you were single again?

Mum: Yes, every morning when I wake up.

Did you hear about the Lottery winner who went on a round-the-world holiday last year?

He says this year he wants to go somewhere else.

A Lottery jackpot winner decided to go on a cruise, and on the first evening, a steward approached him.

'Captain's compliments, sir, and would you like to dine at his table tonight?'

'Get lost,' said the man, 'I didn't spend all this money just to eat with the crew.'

Horace: Do you want to hear a great knock-knock joke?
Herbert: Yes please.
Horace: OK, you start.

Son: Have you and Dad got anything in common, Mum?
Mum: Well, we were married on the same day.

Why was the pirate good at boxing?

He had a great left hook.

DAD
STAT

65% of Dads admit to using their kid's Winnie the Pooh soft toy as an emergency demister in the car.

Son: Athletics at school tomorrow, Dad.

Dad: Athletics? In the middle of winter! Are you sure?

Son: Yes, the head will be back and teacher said when she is we're all for the high jump.

Doctor: Right, first I want you to lean out of the window and stick out your tongue.

Patient: Will that help you diagnose me?

Doctor: No, I just don't like the man who lives over the road.

Did you hear about the man who lived in a car tyre?

He had a puncture and now he lives in a flat.

A flea came across a spider suspended from a dog's knee.
He asked him, 'What are you doing hanging around this joint?'

Did you hear about the idiot who collapsed after winning a marathon?
He was fine at the finish, but the lap of honour finished him off.

Lady to man reading poetry: Tell me, do you enjoy Kipling?
Man: I don't know, I've never been kippled.

First man: I slept
like a log last night.
Second man:
That's good.
First man: Not really,
I woke up in the fireplace.

**What's a crocodile's
favourite game?**
Snap!

Coach: Now the important thing before this big
race is not to be nervous.
Athlete: I'm not nervous. It's them that should be
nervous. What makes you think I'm nervous?
Coach: You've got your trainers on the wrong feet.

A woman was
in a library
when she saw
a man playing
chess with a dog.

**Patient: Doctor, I'm
allergic to pantomimes.**
Doctor: Oh no you're not.

'That's one clever dog,' she said to the man.
'Not really,' said the man. 'I win more than
he does.'

Two mathematicians had been struggling to work out the height of a long pole leaning against a wall.

Eventually an engineer came by and offered to help. He took hold of the pole, lay it on the ground and measured it with a tape.

'Typical engineer,' said the mathematicians. 'We wanted the height and he gave us the length.'

God and Satan are in dispute about the boundary between heaven and hell. Eventually God threatens to take Satan to court.

'Oh yes,' said Satan, 'and where are you going to find a lawyer?'

What did the Dalek who worked at the beauty parlour say?
'Ex-fol-i-ate! Ex-fol-i-ate!'

Son: Dad always seems happy, doesn't he, Mum.

Mum: Well, they do say 'ignorance is bliss'.

Customer: I just played this record and all I could hear was a loud buzzing.
Record-shop assistant: Ah, you must have been playing the B-side.

Bertha took her friend Sheila to the bingo for the first time. But she got fed up as Sheila kept leaning over and telling her when to cross off the numbers. Eventually she lost her temper.
'Why don't you just mark up your own card, Sheila?'
'Oh, mine's been full for the last five minutes.'

What did Obi Wan-Kenobi say to Luke Skywalker when he kept eating with his fingers?
Use the fork, Luke!

What starts with 𝕿 ends with 𝕿 and is full of 𝕿?

A teapot.

A drummer decides to learn a proper instrument and goes to a music shop. After much deliberation, he says, 'I'll have that red trumpet and the accordion by the wall.'

The shop owner says, 'I can sell you the fire extinguisher if you like, but the radiator will have to stay.'

What has eight legs and smells of pine?

A spider in a Radox bath.

Colonel: Pass me the ice cream, Private.

Private: I can't, sir.

Colonel: Why not?!

Private: The sergeant says it's against regulations to help other soldiers to dessert.

What do you call a woman with dental thread all over her?

Floss.

What do you get if you cross a whale with an elephant?
A submarine with a built-in snorkel.

What do you give a worn-out bunny?
Hare restorer.

First man: I had to go and work abroad for six months, and wrote to my girlfriend every day.
Second man: And what happened?
First man: She married the postman.

Why did the useless golfer's wife have him buried beneath his own father?
She said at last he'd be under Pa!

Patient: Doctor, I keep feeling flushed.
Doctor: Sounds like some sort of chain reaction.

Two brothers went to enlist in the armed forces.

'Have you got any special skills?' the first one was asked.

'I'm a pilot,' he replied, and was immediately signed up.

Then they asked the other brother the same question. 'I chop wood,' he said. He was rejected.

'But you took my brother on,' he protested.

'Yes, but he's a pilot.'

'Well, he can't pile it until I've chopped it, can he?'

What's a golfer's
favourite deodorant?

Links!

Why was the plastic bag put in
quarantine for six months?

They thought he might be a carrier.

Boy: Isn't it odd that 'Dad' and 'Mum' are both palindromes.
Girl: Not really, they're always saying they don't know if they're coming or going.

First man: I've just seen an amazing bloke. He emptied a toolbox and chopped them all into little pieces using only his teeth.
Second man: That's incredible. Was he a professional strongman?
First man: No, just a hammer-chewer.

Cold caller: Can I give you a price to trim your hedge?
Householder: Well, it does need doing badly.
Cold caller: Then I'm just the man you need.

How did Moses see in the desert at night?
He switched on the Israelites.

First man: I thought you were going to the clairvoyant today?

Second man: I was, but when I got there it said, 'Closed due to unforeseen circumstances.'

A man went into a pub and order six double whiskies. When they arrived he downed them all in seconds, one after the other.

'Hang on,' said the barman, 'what's the rush?'

'You'd drink quickly if you had what I've got,' said the customer.

'Oh dear, what have you got?' asked the barman.

'Fifty pence.'

> **What did one mayfly say to another mayfly?**
>
> Have a nice day!

First man: I'm fed up with being single.

Second man: Have you tried computer dating?

First man: Who wants to go out with a computer?

Did you hear about the man who bought a pair of tortoiseshell shoes?
It took him two hours to get out of the shop.

Herbert: What have you got in that bag?
Horace: Cabbages.
Herbert: If I can guess how many there are, can I have one?
Horace: If you can do that, I'll give you both of them.

Dad: If I die first, I don't mind at all if you want to get married again – just don't let him wear my clothes!

Mum: Don't worry, they don't fit him…

Fortune-teller: Someone near you is going to be disappointed soon.

Customer: That'll be you – I've come out without my wallet.

Dad: That new barber's going to get plenty of customers with his latest offer.

Mum: What latest offer?

Dad: It says, 'Hair cut while you wait'.

Supermarket assistant: Can I help you, sir?

Man: I know I was sent here for a casserole or a camisole but I can't remember which.

Assistant: Well, sir, is the bird dead or alive?

Judge: You are charged with murdering a man with sandpaper. How do you plead?

Defendant: Not guilty, your honour – I only meant to rough him up a bit.

Mum: Don't you ever use a lavatory brush?

Dad: No, I find the paper much softer.

Customer: Are you sure this car only had one previous owner?

Salesman: Definitely, sir.

Customer: Who was it, Queen Victoria?

> **How do you console a friend?**
>
> Give them an X-Box.

Son: Are the TV adverts right to say it wouldn't be Christmas without M&S?

Dad: I suppose so – without them it would just be Chrita.

Son: Dad, if bigamy is having one wife too many, what's monogamy?
Dad: Pretty much
the same.

First idiot: Christmas Day is going to be on a Friday this year.
Second idiot: Let's hope it's not the 13th then.

Where do napkins come from?

The Serviette Union.

Why did the Olympic rowing champion retire?

He got fed up of all the arguing.

Man in bar: I see your glass is empty – would you like another?
Woman: What would I want with two empty glasses?

Did you hear what happened to the really unlucky teetotal dyslexic?
He choked on his own Vimto.

What do you give the man who has everything?
An intensive course of antibiotics.

What's the best way to serve turkey?
Join the Turkish Army.

Have you heard about the latest on the government's happiness index?
In a recent survey, six out of seven dwarfs said they were not happy.

Patient: What's the prognosis, doc?
Doctor: Well, I wouldn't bother buying any green bananas if I were you.

The vicar was strolling round his parish when he came upon old Joe tending his lovely garden.

'Isn't it wonderful, Joe,' he said, 'to see what beauty man and the Lord can achieve when they work together.'

'I suppose so,' said Joe, 'but you should have seen the state of it a few years ago when God was looking after it on his own.'

Who are cleverer, gardeners or farmers?

Farmers – they have hay levels but gardeners only have hoe levels.

Mavis was bored in the old folks home, fed up with the routine. In an act of liberation she took all her clothes off and streaked through the garden, past a surprised Bert and Fred on the bench.

'Was that Mavis?' asked Bert.

'I think so,' said Fred.

'What was she wearing?'

'I don't know, but it needed a good ironing.'

> **Why is a lamppost heavy at the bottom?**
>
> Because it's light at the top.

Idiot: Hello, is that Birmingham 3054781?

Man: No, this is Birmingham 3054782.

Idiot: Oh, well could you nip next door and tell them I'm on the phone.

Pupil: I think Santa is stupid.

Teacher: Why do you say that?

Pupil: Because we've got two doors and eight windows in our house and he still comes down the chimney.

What's big, grey and runs away from the ball?

Cinderellaphant.

Why are bibles like squirrels?

There are millions of them but very few are red.

What do you call a man with a pole through his leg?
Rodney.

What's white, square and heavy and wears a checked scarf?
Rupert the Fridge.

How long does it take to buy a Mexican dog?
Chihuahuas.

Son: Why did you give Mum a wooden leg for Christmas?
Dad: I thought it would be a good stocking filler.

The richest, stupidest man on the planet, who is obsessed with space travel, has announced plans to send a rocket to the sun.
When asked if it wouldn't be too hot, he answered that he'd thought of that, and he was going to go at night.

Man: Every time the doorbell rings our dog runs into a corner.

Vet: Well, of course he does, he's a boxer.

First man: It's a nice house, but you haven't got a clock anywhere.

Second man: No, I just use my trumpet.

First man: How do you tell the time with your trumpet?

Second man: Well, I play it in the middle of the night and my neighbour opens his window and shouts, 'What do you mean playing that thing at two o'clock in the morning!'

Doctor: I don't know what you expect me to do for you just because you're scared of Father Christmas.

Patient: I didn't say I was scared of Father Christmas, I said I'd got claustrophobia!

Teacher: Can you all hear the fire alarm?

Pupil: Is it a drill, sir?

Teacher: No, you idiot, it's a bell.

First tree: Have you worked out yet when the lumberjacks are going to get here?

Second tree: No, I'm completely stumped.

Why couldn't the owl go out with his girlfriend in the rain?

Because it was too wet to woo.

Why can't pigs talk to one another on the phone?

There's too much crackling.

Why is it so difficult to teach dogs to dance?

They've got two left feet.

What do you give
a reindeer with
indigestion?

Elk-a-seltzer.

What cheese do
you use to entice
Paddington out
of his house?
Camembert.

Mum: What were you doing last night in bed?
You kept shouting about hobbits and elves.
Dad: Sorry, I must have been Tolkien in my sleep.

What sentence would you get for breaking the
law of gravity?
A suspended one.

Mum: I saw my old boyfriend last night –
apparently he hasn't stopped drinking since
I broke up with him ten years ago.
Dad: Fair enough, but you'd have thought
he'd have stopped celebrating by now.

What did the scientist say when a lump of gold jumped onto his Periodic Table?
AU, get off my table!

Why wouldn't the alligator's car start?

It was a old croc.

A news-seller was standing on the corner, shouting, 'Read all about it! Twenty people swindled! Twenty people swindled!'
A man going past bought a newspaper from him and started leafing through it. 'Hang on,' he said to the seller, 'there's nothing in here about a swindle.'
'Read all about! Twenty-one people swindled!'

Teacher: Just for once, I'd like to go through the day without telling you off, Jimmy.
Jimmy: That's fine by me, miss, why don't you give it a try.

How does old MacDonald communicate?

Via e-i-e-i-o-mail.

Pearls of Fatherly Wisdom

1. Bacon and eggs – a day's work for the chicken, a lifetime commitment for the pig

2. He who laughs last ... has no sense of humour

3. If a man says something and no woman is around to hear him ... is he still wrong?

4. People who live in glass houses should put the toilet in the cellar

5. The early bird gets the worm, but the second mouse gets the cheese

6. I could agree with you but then we'd both be wrong

7. A friend in need is a flippin' nuisance

8. If you can keep your head when all around are losing theirs ... you obviously haven't realised how serious the situation is

9. Be alert! Britain needs lerts!

10. The sooner I fall behind, the more time I'll have to catch up

Old man: I was born in 1975.

Nurse: I don't think you were, dear.

Old man: Yes I was, it was right next door to room 1974.

First kangeroo: I hope it doesn't rain today.

Second kangeroo: Why?

First kangeroo: The kids will want to play inside again.

Teacher: Does anyone know what a bachelor is?

Pupil: My Dad says it's someone who never makes the same mistake once.

Teacher: What was the first fruit mentioned in the Bible?

Johnny: A pear, miss.

Teacher: No, Johnny, it was an apple, eaten by Adam and Eve.

Johnny: Yes, but Adam and Eve were a pair.

Dad: As it's Mother's Day, I took your Mum a cup of tea this morning in my pyjamas.

Son: I bet that surprised her.

Dad: It did, but she said next time she'd prefer it in a cup.

Teacher: Complete the proverb, 'One good turn...'

Pupil: Gets most of the quilt.

A journalist was being shown around the most hi-tech computer centre in the world by its owner.

'It's so advanced we only employ one man and one dog,' said the owner.

'What's the man's job?' asked the reporter.

'To feed the dog.'

'So what's the dog's job?'

'He's there to stop the man touching the computer.'

Dad: Did you like the bird I sent you for Christmas, Mum?
Gran: Yes, it was delicious.
Dad: Delicious! But it was rare African parrot, highly trained, it spoke three languages!
Gran: Well, it should have said something when I put it in the oven.

Jimmy: Don't tell Mum, but I had a fight with the school bully today.
Jane: Oh no, what happened?
Jimmy: Well, after a couple of minutes I had him worried.
Jane: Really?!
Jimmy: Yes, he thought he'd killed me.

Teacher: What is a humanitarian?

Rodney: A cannibal.

Teacher: What on earth makes you think that?

Rodney: Well, a vegetarian eats vegetables.

First man: When I was ten I ran away with a circus.

Second man: Wow, what happened?

First man: They made me bring it back.

Tramp: Will you give me £1.50 for a sandwich?

Man: No thanks, I'm not hungry.

Headmaster: I don't like caning you, Jones. In fact, this is hurting me far more than it's hurting you.

Jones: Is that really true, sir?

Headmaster: Most definitely.

Jones: In that case, sir, please carry on and don't mind me.

Jimmy: Miss, do you know why the Army have called their new gun 'the teacher'.

Teacher: No, why?

Jimmy: Because it doesn't work and can't be fired.

Dad: I've had it with that place. The boss said two words to me today that make it impossible for me to work there ever again.

Mum: What did he say?

Dad: 'You're sacked'.

Fred: Are you going to Charlie's funeral?

Bert: I don't think so – he's not going to come to mine, is he?

Jane: Why do you call your cat Ben Hur?

Jill: Well, we used to just call it Ben, but then it had kittens.

Herbert: I haven't seen Jim lately.

Horace: No, he won a trip to Australia in a competition.

Herbert: That's terrific.

Horace: Not really, he's still out there, trying to win a trip back.

First man: I went to the opera last night, and I couldn't believe how stuck up everyone is.

Second man: Really?

First man: Yes, they get really snotty when you start to sing along.

Mum: Why have we come here on holiday? It must be the crummiest, dirtiest, most boring seaside town in Britain.

Dad: I tried to book somewhere else, but this was the last resort.

What do you get from a pampered cow?

Spoiled milk.

A mechanic, a priest and an IT guy are in a car when all of a sudden it slows to a halt.

The mechanic says: 'That sounds to me like we've run out of petrol.'

The priest says: 'I think we should all say a prayer.'

The IT guy says: 'I think we should close all open windows, then get out of the car and get back in again.'

An idiot is walking along a river bank, wondering how to get across. On the opposite bank he sees another idiot.

'Hey,' he shouts, 'how can I get to the other side?'

'You're already on the other side!' comes the reply.

What should you do if you run over a chicken in a truck?
Make coq-au-vin.

What's a boxer's favourite part of a joke?

The punch line.

Why don't blind people skydive?
It scares the dog too much.

How do you make a stupid man's eyes light up?
Shine a torch in his ear.

Barman: Yes, sir, what'll it be?
Skeleton: A pint of bitter and a mop, please.

What's the difference between a trampoline and a set of bagpipes?
You take your shoes off before jumping on a trampoline.

Did you hear about the man in the health food shop who was killed when a display of vitamins and herbal extracts fell on him?
The coroner said he died of natural causes.

Dad: Can you pop down to the corner shop for me?
Son: No problem, how many corners do you want?

Therapist: I think the answer to your drink problem would be a frontal lobotomy.
Patient: I'd rather have a bottle in front of me.

What's nosy and ticks?
The neighbourhood watch.

Did you hear about the idiot who wouldn't go house-hunting?
He said he hadn't got a big enough gun.

Someone has broken into the headquarters of North Korea's government offices.
Nothing was stolen apart from next year's election results.

Man: Officer, come quickly, there's a man wandering round St James's Park asking everyone how to get to Downing Street so he can shoot the Prime Minister.
Policeman: Well, can't someone else tell him?

First woman: I hear all your family are grown-up now.
Second woman: Well, all except my husband...

Teacher: I'm not as stupid as I look.
Pupil: No, nobody could be that stupid.

Why were Tinkerbell's wings tired?
Because all the signs around her said 'Never Land'.

Pupil: I've been sent to watch the sex-education film.
Teacher: OK, do you want to sit in smirking or non-smirking?

How do you get a student into the shower?

Put a beer in it.

In the woods, a little squirrel kept throwing himself off a tree branch, flapping his legs furiously. Every time he crashed to the ground, and every time he would climb back up and jump off again.

Two birds were watching the scene, and eventually one turned to the other and said, 'I think it's time we told him he was adopted.'

Boss: I've heard about the effort you're putting in for your department.
Trainee: Oh, it's nothing.
Boss: Yes, that's what I've heard.

Did you hear about the hearse-driver who fancied a change after twenty years and became a taxi-driver instead?

He crashed the car on his first day when a passenger tapped him on the shoulder.

Mum: I should have known me and your Dad were incompatible.

Son: Why?

Mum: Well, I'm a Scorpio and he's a lazy, immature twit.

Why do old people read the Bible so much?

They're cramming for their finals.

A man went to see a lawyer and asked him what his fee was.

'I charge £500 for three questions,' said the lawyer.

'Isn't that a bit greedy?' asked the man.

'Yes it is, what's your final question?'

A racehorse owner was disgusted with how his horse had run and went to find the jockey after the race to bawl him out.

'Could you not have gone any faster?' he demanded.

'Well I could have,' said the jockey, 'but I had to stay on the horse.'

A little old lady goes to see her doctor.

'Doctor, I can't stop breaking wind. Thank goodness they don't make a noise and they don't smell, but it goes on all day long.'

'Well,' says the doctor, 'take these tablets and come back in a week.'

A week later she's back.

'I don't know what was in those tablets, doctor, I'm still breaking wind silently but now they smell awful.'

'Right,' says the doctor, 'now we've sorted out your sinuses we'll see what we can do about your hearing.'

> How do you get a student out of the shower?
>
> Turn it on.

Teacher: **You're living proof that light travels faster than sound.**

Pupil: Why, miss?

Teacher: **Well, I thought you looked bright until I heard you speak.**

Hebert and Horace are walking down a street when Herbert finds a mirror and picks it up.

He looks into it and says, 'Hey, this bloke looks familiar.'

Horace takes it off him, looks into it, and says, 'Of course it is, you fool, it's me!'

Son: **Dad, should I wait to meet Miss Right before I get married?**

Dad: Well I did, son. I just wish I'd realised her first name was 'Always'.

What goes, 'clip, clip'?

A horse with two legs.

> **What happened to the idiot who took up ice-fishing?**
>
> He got thrown out of the skating rink.

Teacher: Jimmy, can you name something that's good for your health?

Jimmy: Birthdays, miss.

Teacher: Why do you say that?

Jimmy: Well, the more you have, the longer you live.

Boss: Are you going to take your pay cheque to the bank?

Employee: I certainly am, it's too small to go by itself.

Patient: Doctor, I think I've got athlete's voice.

Doctor: Don't you mean athlete's foot?

Patient: No, every time I sing, people run away.

A man was at the Cup Final and was surprised to see an empty seat beside him. He asked the man on the other side of the seat if he knew whose it was.

'Well,' said the man, 'my wife and I have always wanted to come to the Cup Final, and this year we finally managed to get tickets. But unfortunately, recently she was run over by a bus and died.'

'That's awful,' said the first man. 'But isn't there a friend or relation could have come with you?'

'No, they're all at the funeral.'

What's the difference between a weasel and a stoat?

A weasel is weaselly identified and a stoat is stoatally different.

Why is a bad boxer like a postage stamp?

He keeps getting licked and put in the corner.

Mum: My mother was criticising you today but I stuck up for you.

Dad: Thanks, love, what happened?

Mum: She said you weren't fit to sleep in a pigsty, but I said you were.

Mum: You've just heard my daughter playing Brahms. What do you think of her execution?

Piano-teacher: I'm in favour of it.

Two drunks were on a train as it pulled into a station.

One said, 'Is this Wembley?'

The other said, 'No, it's Thursday.'

'So am I, let's go for a drink.'

Passenger: Is this bug going to Dagenham?

Driver: I don't think so, it's never daggened anyone yet.

Teacher: Bobby, did you believe me yesterday when I told you there were billions and billions of stars in the universe?

Bobby: Yes, miss.

Teacher: So why did you feel the need to check when I told you there was wet paint on the playground bench?

DAD STAT

The average blood pressure of a Dad who has just been given his first quote for adding his 17-year-old to his car insurance is 155 over 100.

A lady decided she wanted to bathe in milk,
so she rang the Co-op up to arrange a delivery.
'Do you want it pasteurised?' they asked.
'No, as long as it comes up to my chest,
it'll be fine.'

First woman: My husband plays for a Welsh
football team.
Second woman: Wrexham?
First woman: Well, he's not very good.

What's the best thing out?

A sore tooth.

First man: Since I met my wife, I've turned my
life around.
Second man: How do you mean?
First man: Well, before I met her I was miserable
and depressed. Now I'm depressed and miserable.

Mum: What are you
going to do today?
Dad: Nothing.
Mum: But you did
that yesterday.
Dad: I know, but
I haven't finished yet.

How do you
communicate
with a fish?

Drop it a line.

What did the snail say when it rode on the
tortoise's back?
Weeeeeeeeeeeeeeeee!!!!!!!!!

Son: Mum, I don't like the holes in this Swiss
cheese.
Mum: Well, eat the cheese and leave the holes on
the side of your plate.

What's the hardest train to catch?
The 12:50, because it's only ten to one you'll catch it.

Charlie: My dog bit me on the leg last week.

Albert: Did you put anything on it?

Charlie: No, he liked it fine just the way it was.

Dad: What would you like for your birthday? A Rolex? A sports car?

Mum: A divorce!

Dad: I wasn't thinking of spending that much.

Teacher: What did you do at the weekend, Billy?

Billy: Me and my dog went for a tramp in the woods.

Teacher: That sounds lovely.

Billy: It was great, but the tramp didn't think much of it.

**Man in dentist: I love this new chair you've got –
it's great the way it goes in and out instead of
up and down.**
Dentist: Will you please get out of my filing cabinet!

**Son: Dad looks lost in
thought, Mum.**
Mum: I'm not
surprised – he's never
been there before.

**Best man: It's
been such a perfect
wedding that even
the cake is in tiers!**

**First worm: Have you seen those two maggots
fighting?**
Second worm: Are they just messing around?
First worm: No, they're in dead Ernest.

**What's the difference between Joan of Arc and
Noah's Ark?**
Joan of Arc was Maid of Orleans and Noah's Ark
was made of wood.

As an experiment
I took both sides
off my ladder.
I didn't like it, now
it just looks rung.

Where do the
trendy young bees
go to congratulate
one another?

Hive five!

Did you hear the
joke about the
marathon runner
who ran into a
hairdresser's ...
and asked for
a shortcut!

First woman: How
did the trial
separation go?
Second woman:
It worked –
I haven't seen him
for 18 months!

First man: I've just discovered the biggest piece
of round black vinyl ever made.
Second man: Wow, that must be some kind of record.

Why can't steam engines sit down?
Because they have a tender behind!

What do they call
an upside-down
cake in Australia?
A cake.

Passenger: Is this bus going to Clapham?
Driver: Only if they're very good.

Dad: What do you mean, I'm an underachiever?
Mum: Well, when Mozart was your age he'd already
been dead for ten years.

**Son: Why has the wood in that cupboard
you're building got holes in?**
Dad: They're knot holes.
Son: Well, if they're not holes, what are they?

What are a dentist's favourite two letters?
DK.

What's the difference between a tub of lard and a teacher?

One's a good lot of fat and the other's a fat lot of good.

Elsie and Flo were standing at a bus-stop:

Elsie: See that man on the other side of the road. He must be the ugliest, rudest, laziest man in town.

Flo: That's my husband, actually.

Elsie: Oh, I'm sorry.

Flo: *You're* sorry?!

Doctor: Why have you brought your baby to see me?

Mum: He's a funny colour.

Doctor: He looks fine to me.

Mum: Yes, but at night he becomes a horrible yeller.

Teacher: What is a fjord?

Pupil: Is it a Norwegian car?

Jimmy was helping his Dad with some D-I-Y.

'You're like lightning with that hammer, Jimmy,' said Dad.

'Fast, am I?' asked Jimmy.

'No, it's just you never strike twice in the same place.'

What's it like being a trampolinist?

It has its ups and downs.

What happens if you play table tennis with a rotten egg?
First it goes ping, and then it goes pong!

Herbert had been visiting Horace, but when he came to leave there was a violent storm in progress.

'You can't go out in this storm,' said Horace. 'Why don't you stay the night?'

'That's very kind of you,' said Herbert, 'I'll just pop home and get my pyjamas.'

> **Customer: How long will my pizza be?**
> Waiter: It won't be long, it'll be round.

How did Benjamin Franklin invent electricity?
It came to him in a flash.

Customer: Is this a second-hand shop?
Shopkeeper: Yes.
Customer: Good, can you fit one to my watch?

Did you hear about the idiots' tug-o-war team?
They were disqualified for pushing.

Police surrounded a bank yesterday while an armed raid was going on, and secured all the exits.
The robbers then escaped through one of the entrances.

Why did the stupid criminal saw the legs off his bed?

He wanted to lie low for a while.

What is the longest piece of furniture in a school?

The multiplication table.

What happened to the naughty chicken?

He was eggspelled.

Dad: I'm in trouble with Mum again.

Son: Why?

Dad: Well, she's got laryngitis so I thought I'd buy her some chocolate to cheer her up.

Son: So?

Dad: I bought her a Wispa.

Diner: I didn't order rabbit pie, young man!

Waiter: It isn't rabbit pie, sir, it's steak and kidney.

Diner: Well, what about all these hares in it?

It was the hottest day of the year and the teacher came into the classroom sweating.

'Ninety-one today, children, can you believe it?'

'Happy birthday to you, Happy birthday to you...'

Maths teacher: Why haven't you done your homework on decimals, Tommy?

Tommy: I couldn't see the point, sir.

What did the cheese say to the mirror?

Halloumi!

Customer: Would you like to sell twice as much beer as you do now?

Landlord: I certainly would.

Customer: Then fill up the flippin' glasses!

Your mum's face looks like a million dollars.

All green and wrinkly.

Music teacher: If 'f' means 'forte', what does 'ff' mean?
Pupil: Eighty?

The god of thunder was out for a ride on his favourite horse, the wind rushing through his hair.
'I'm Thor!!!' he cried, to no one in particular.
'Well,' said his horse, 'you forgot your thaddle, thilly!'

First man: My dog's always chasing people on bicycles.
Second man: Well, take his bicycles away then.

What type of animal is a camelemac?

A palindromedary.

Harry: My budgie died of flu yesterday, miss.
Teacher: Was it bird flu?
Harry: No, he flew into the lawnmower.

First cat: How did you do in the milk-drinking contest?

Second cat: I won by two laps.

Mum: Wake up! Someone's broken in downstairs and he's in the kitchen eating that cake I made. Dial 999.

Dad: Who shall I ask for – police or ambulance?

First scientist: My desk keeps disappearing and coming back.

Second scientist: Ah, you must have a periodic table.

First man: Your mother-in-law died quite suddenly – what was the complaint?

Second man: We haven't had any yet.

How do mountains hear things?

With their mountain-ears.

What does a hippy do?
Stops your leggy from falling off.

Pupil: Miss, if the blood rushes to my head when I stand upside down, why doesn't it rush to my feet when I stand the right way up?
Teacher: Because your feet aren't empty.

Doctor: Now, how's your broken rib coming along?
Patient: Well, I've started getting a stitch in my side.
Doctor: Good, that means the bone is knitting.

Patient: Doctor, I think I'm invisible.

Doctor: Well, you're certainly not all there.

First man: What's the best way to Manchester?

Second man: Are you walking or driving?

First man: Driving.

Second man: Good, that's the best way.

Grandpa: I've got a brilliant new hearing aid, all-digital, it's perfect.

Dad: Sounds marvellous, what type is it?

Grandpa: Half-past four.

Why wouldn't the Egyptian believe he was drowning?

He was in denial!

Customer: Is that a doughnut or a meringue?

Baker: You're right, it's a doughnut.

Mum: What's that lion and witch doing in your wardrobe?

Son: It's Narnia business.

Patient: Doctor, can you give me anything to keep my hair in?

Doctor: How about this little box?

Mum: When are you going to put those shelves up?

Dad: Stop nagging, I've said I'll do it and I will – you don't have to keep asking me every six months.

> **What's white and square?**
>
> A ping-pong cube.

First man: Why did you give up your job as a taxi-driver?

Second man: I got fed up with people talking behind my back.

Teacher: How often do you do your homework, Billy?
Billy: Almost every day, miss.
Teacher: I find that hard to believe.
Billy: Oh, yes, almost on Monday, almost on Tuesday, almost on Wednesday …

What's green and not very heavy?
Light green.

Teacher: That was a very interesting talk by the local undertaker. Does anyone have any questions?
Pupil: Why do you nail down the lids on coffins?

Butcher: Would you like some cured ham?
Customer: It depends what it was cured of.

Patient: Doctor, I keep thinking I'm a rucksack.
Doctor: Well, don't go rambling on to me about it.

Herbert: Can I buy a green Union Jack please?

Shopkeeper: I'm sorry, they only come in red, white and blue.

Herbert: All right, I'll have a blue one.

Divorce judge: Mr Smith, I have decided to award your wife £200 per week.

Smith: That's very good of you, your honour. I'll try and slip her a few quid myself when I'm flush.

Little boy at carnival: I've lost my Dad.

Policeman: Righto, what's he like?

Little boy: Beer and blondes.

First man: I caught a 10lb fish yesterday.

Second man: Oh yes? Were there any witnesses?

First man: Certainly – if there hadn't been it would have been a 20lb fish.

Horace and Herbert are walking along a road when they see two other men coming towards them with a bag full of huge fish.

'How did you catch them?' asked Horace.

'My friend dangled me over the bridge by my legs and I caught the fish as they swam up river.'

They decide to give it a try. They got to the bridge and Horace lowered Herbert down. He'd been dangling there for five minutes when he shouted, 'Quick, pull me up, pull me up!'

'Have you caught a fish?'

'No, there's a train coming!'

What does the Dentist of the Year receive?

A little plaque.

First doctor: Do you usually keep your rectal thermometer in your breast pocket?

Second doctor: Damn! Some bum's got my Parker.

DAD'S
IDEAL
BAR CHART

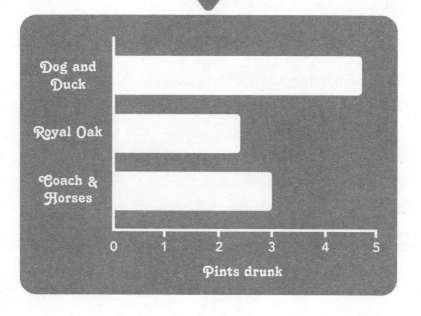

What do you call
pain-free yoghurts?

Yogs.

What did Arnold Schwarzenegger say when his wife asked him if Christmas was his favourite holiday?

I still love Easter, baby!

First pensioner: I think I'm stronger than I was 20 years ago.

Second pensioner: But you're 80 – how do you work that out?

First pensioner: Well, back then I struggled to carry £5-worth of potatoes – now it's quite easy.

How does Long John Silver keep fit?

Gym, lad!

Policeman: Do you know why I've pulled you over, sir?

Motorist: It depends. How long have you been following me?

Baker: Two pies for £1.50, sir?
Customer: How much is that one on its own?
Baker: One pound, sir.
Customer: Here's 50p, I'll have the other one.

Jimmy: My dad says he wants me to have all the educational opportunities he never had.
Eric: So what's he doing?
Jimmy: He's sending me to a girls' school.

A horse goes into a bar and says, 'Can I have a large aperitif, please.'
The barman says, 'They look large enough to me already.'

Scotsman on holiday: What's yon beast over there?
Canadian: That's a moose.
Scotsman: Och, if that's a moose, how big are your cats?

What happened to the two monocles who went on Big Brother?
They made a spectacle of themselves.

Son: Mum, I hate my sister's guts!
Mum: Well, just leave them on the side of your plate.

First man: I've just been violently criticised by a harassed meringue.
Second man: Sounds like you were harangued.

Jack: Did you know Charlie has a glass eye?
Jim: No, how did you find out?
Jack: It just came out in conversation.

98% of Dad's dislike their daughter's first boyfriend no matter how 'lovely and nice' Mum says he is.

DAD STAT

> **Why did the idiot give up drag racing?**
> He couldn't get the crash helmet over his wig.

George: Kelvin, why do all your Christmas cards say 'To Kevin'?
Kelvin: Because there's Nowell at Christmas.

Golf coach: I think I've spotted your problem.
Golfer: What is it?
Coach: You're standing too close to your ball after you've hit it.

First man: I think graffiti should be legalised.
Second man: Well, you should sign a partition.

New teacher: Is it right that you always answer one question with another, Johnny?
Johnny: Who told you that, miss?

Guest: I want to complain about the fleas.

Hotel manager: I'm sure you won't find a single flea in our beds.

Guest: I didn't, they were all married with large families.

Dora: I think my husband's been unfaithful to me.

Flo: Why do you say that?

Dora: Well, my youngest child doesn't look like him at all.

Son: Why is Mum crying?

Dad: I told her that her stockings were a bit wrinkly.

Son: Why did that make her cry?

Dad: She wasn't wearing any.

> **Why did the army use carrier pigeons to plot against the government?**
>
> They wanted to launch a military coo.

Jack: Why isn't Herbert's car working?

Jim: He reversed into a car-boot sale and somebody bought the engine.

Horace: I want a refund on this tie I bought yesterday.

Shopkeeper: What's wrong with it?

Horace: It's too tight.

> **Which sailor works at the Large Hadron Collider?**
>
> Bosun Higgs.

Son: Mum, I've met a lovely girl and we want to get married.

Mum: Mama mia! How can-a you do this-a to your-a dear mamma? You got-a no respect!

Son: You can't talk to me like that, mum.

Mum: Why-a not?

Son: Because you're not Italian.

Son: Mum seems a bit cross with you, Dad.
Dad: It's not my fault. She asked for something silky
for her birthday so I bought her a tin of paint.
Son: Maybe it was the wrong colour...

Man: Hello.
Caller: Is that Mr Graham?
Man: No, you must have the wrong number.
Caller: Well, if it's the wrong number, why did you
answer it?

Sally: Why did you break it off with that tennis player?
Dolly: I had to – love meant nothing to him.

Teacher: Did you read that book about glue, Jimmy?
Jimmy: I couldn't put it down, miss.

Passenger: Is this the Barking bus?
Driver: No, it just goes vroom, vroom.

Apparently a man gets mugged in Central London every ten minutes.
He's getting a bit fed up with it...

Woman: Doctor, my son thinks he's a chicken.
Doctor: Why haven't you brought him in, I'm sure I can do something.
Woman: Yes, but we need the eggs.

> **First robot: Have you got any brothers?**
> Second robot: No, just transistors.

Gran: I'm going home tomorrow – I don't suppose you'll be disappointed.
Dad: Yes I am – I thought you were going today.

Horace and Herbert went to the zoo. Horace threw a stone at a lion, who immediately jumped over the fence and started running towards them.
'Quick, run!' said Horace.
'Why should I run?' said Herbert. 'You threw the rock.'

First man at funeral: I thought he wanted to leave his body to the medical school?
Second man: He did – but the medical school contested the will.

DIGITAL DAD

Typical Dad Texts

1. WT HV U DUN 2 MY CAR?!

2. Y IS YR PHONE ALWYS 'DED' WHEN I CLL U, BT NVR WHEN U WANT A LIFT!

3. AM ABT 2 GO IN YR ROOM - IF NO NEWS IN 1HR PLS CALL 999

4. HV JST BN IN YR ROOM - FND LORD LUCAN

5. NO, FRT GUMS DO NT COUNT AS 1 OF YR 5-A-DAY

6. WR U THNKG OF CMG HOME 2NITE, OR SHL I JST COLLECT U FRM POLICE STATION?

7. DO U BY ANY CHNC KNOW Y THE DOG IS WRG PERFUME?

8. I THNK THT LST TXT U SENT ME WAS MEANT 4 YR GFND! (DON'T WORRY, I HV SAVED IT....)

9. I DON'T CR IF JIM'S DAD IS 'COOL WITH IT', UR NT GNG TO AMSTERDAM

10. WHERE HV U PUT THE REMOTE? FOOTY IS ABT 2 START!

Two men sitting next to each other on a plane **strike up a conversation and start swapping jokes.** 'I've got a brilliant teacher joke,' says one. **'I'd better let you know,' said the other, 'I'm a teacher myself.'** 'Don't worry,' said the other, 'I'll tell it really slowly.'

First diner: I'll have a mineral water, please. Second diner: Same for me, and make sure it's in a clean glass. **Waiter (returning with drinks): Which one of you wanted the clean glass?**

Gran cut two slices of cake and offered the plate to little Jimmy, who helped himself to the large piece. 'Now, Jimmy, if I'd been offered first choice, I'd have chosen the smaller piece,' said Gran. **'That's OK then, that's the piece you've got,' replied Jimmy.**

Policeman: I have pulled you over for erratic driving. Have you been drinking, sir?

Motorist: Let's see, I had a couple of snifters before setting out, three bottles of wine over dinner, two brandies afterwards and (hic) four pints of best bitter before leaving.

Policeman: I'll have to ask you to take a breathalyser test, sir.

Motorist: Why, don't you believe me?

Woman: Are you a policeman?

Man: No, I'm a plain-clothes detective.

Woman: Then why are you wearing a uniform?

Man: It's my day off.

Jack: I just used my donor card at the ATM instead of my bank card.

Jim: What happened?

Jack: It cost me an arm and a leg.

Why aren't there any good nightclubs on the moon?

There's no atmosphere there.

A trainee on his first day was standing by the office shredder with a piece of paper in his hand, looking puzzled, so a secretary asked him what was the matter.

'I don't know how to work this machine, but the boss says this is really urgent,' he said.

'It's quite easy, I'll show you,' said the secretary, taking the paper and feeding it into the shredder. 'Oh, thanks,' said the trainee, 'I just need two copies...'

How do we know Moses was a Dad?
He was lost in the wilderness for forty years and never asked for directions once.

What did the judge say to the dentist?

Do you promise to pull the tooth, the whole tooth, and nothing but the tooth?

Teacher: What can you tell me about probability, Johnny?
Johnny: My dad says, if there's a fifty-fifty chance of something going wrong, then nine times out of ten it will.

An idiot checks into a hotel and five minutes later rings down to reception.

'I can't get out of my room,' he says in a panic.

'Well, just use the door you came in by,' suggested the receptionist.

'I can't, it's got a DO NOT DISTURB sign on it.'

Diner: Waiter, there's a fly in my soup.

Waiter: Drat! I always miss one.

A chimpanzee is sitting in his cage at the zoo reading the Bible and Darwin's Origin of Species.

'Why are you reading those books?' asks his friend.

'I want to find out if I'm my brother's keeper or my keeper's brother,' replied the chimp.

Stewardess: Would you like dinner, sir?

Passenger: What are my choices?

Stewardess: Yes or no.

Terrorists hijacked a plane
full of international bankers.
They issued a statement
saying that they would
release one banker every hour
until their demands were met.

Headmaster: Are you all right, Billy?

Billy: Not really, sir. I've just had measles, tonsillitis, laryngitis, psoriasis and appendicitis.

Headmaster: Dear me, are you sure you should have come to school today?

Billy: I wish I hadn't, I hate Miss Smith's spelling tests.

New boy: Isn't the head a pompous twit!

Girl: Do you know who I am?

Boy: No.

Girl: I'm the head's daughter.

Boy: Oh. Do you know who I am?

Girl: No.

Boy: Good.

Defending lawyer: How many post mortems have you carried out on dead people?
Pathologist: All of them.

Doctor: Nurse, did you take Mr Smith's temperature?
Nurse: I didn't even know it was missing.

A man went into a chemist's and asked if they had anything for hiccups. The assistant immediately slapped him round the face.
'What did you do that for?' asked the man.
'You're not hiccupping now, are you?' said the assistant.
'No, but my wife outside in the car is.'

Station announcer: The train now arriving at platforms 3, 4, 5 and 6 has been derailed and is coming in sideways.

Patient: How much to remove my tooth?

Dentist: £200.

Patient: And how long will it take?

Dentist: About ten minutes.

Patient: £200 for ten minutes!

Dentist: I can make it last an hour if you'd prefer.

What do you call a fox sweeping up herbs?

Basil Brush.

> **Watership Down. You've read the book, you've seen the film, now eat the stew.**

A man rings the maternity hospital:

Man: My wife's nine months pregnant and her contractions are five minutes apart.

Midwife: Is this her first child?

Man: No, you fool, this is her husband.

A doctor had tried everything he knew to cure
his patient's mystery illness. Finally, he said,
'Go home, take a long hot bath, then run round
your garden naked for an hour.'
'But it's the middle of winter,' said the patient, 'I'll
catch pneumonia.'
'Exactly,' said the doctor, 'and I know how to cure
pneumonia.'

Musician: Did you hear my last performance?
Critic: I hope so.

Man at door: I've come to tune your piano.
Woman: But I haven't called a piano tuner.
Man: No, but your neighbour did.

Patient: I spend every night in the pub instead of with my wife, and it makes me feel guilty and depressed.

Psychiatrist: Why can't you stop going to the pub?

Patient: I don't want to stop going, I just want you to stop me feeling guilty and depressed about it.

Hotel guest: Can you send up a bath towel, please.

Receptionist: It'll just be a few minutes, sir, someone else is using it at the moment.

Patient: My wife thinks I'm mad because I like sausages.

Doctor: I'm sure you're not mad – I love sausages.

Patient: Really? You must come and see my collection – I've got hundreds.

Employee: How do I stand for a pay rise?
Boss: You don't stand, you kneel.

How do you de-ice a cloud?
Use a skyscraper.

Son: Why did you say computers were like husbands?
Mum: Because as soon as you choose one, you realise if you'd waited a bit longer you could have had a much better model.

Jobseeker: I see you're looking for labourers. How much do you pay?
Employer: I'll pay you what you're worth.
Jobseeker: No way. I'm not working for that sort of lousy money.

Why do mathematicians get Christmas and Halloween mixed up?
Because DEC 25 = OCT 31.

Boss: I see you've asked for a pay rise. What makes you think I should give you one?
Man: Well, I have three other companies after me.
Boss: Really? Which three?
Man: The gas company, the electric company and the phone company.

Station announcer:
Will the passengers who took the 17:34 to Chipping Norton please bring it back.

Interviewer: Where were you educated?
Candidate: Yale.
Interviewer: Excellent. And what's your name?
Candidate: Yames Yones.

Mum: Do you want the good news or the bad news?

Dad: What's the good news?

Mum: The airbags work on the car.

Customer: How much are your strawberries?

Grocer: £4 per kilo.

> ¶f the answer is '9W', what is the question?
>
> 'Tell me, Mr Wagner, do you spell your name with a V?'

Customer: But the grocer down the street sells them for £2 per kilo, but he hasn't got any today.

Grocer: Well, when I haven't got any in, mine will only be £2 per kilo.

Patient: I've just trodden on a watch and it really hurts.

Doctor: Well, it would – after all, time wounds all heels.

Jimmy: You know you told me that when Dad annoys you, you tell him exactly what you think of him?

Jane: Yes.

Jimmy: Well, I did that yesterday and he stopped my pocket money and grounded me for a week.

Jane: Gosh, you didn't tell him to his face, did you?

Doctor: How's that patient coming along who swallowed all those coins?

Nurse: No change yet, I'm afraid.

What do you call a cravat made out of bacon?

A pigsty.

Eric: Why do you put your hand up every time teacher asks the class a question?

Jimmy: Well, by the time I get back from the toilet, someone else has answered it.

Diner: I ordered my meal half an hour ago. What are you waiting for?
Waiter: £5 an hour plus tips.

What do you call a rabbit with fleas?

Bugs Bunny.

Customer: Do you sell brassieres?
Sales assistant: Certainly, madam, what bust?
Customer: One of the straps.

Charlie: How was your holiday?
Bert: We felt on top of the world.
Charlie: That good?
Bert: That cold!

Why are there so many Smiths in the telephone directory?
Because they all have telephones.

Why did the Red Indian wear a woolly hat?
To keep his wigwam.

What happened to the man who fell into an upholstery machine?
He's fully recovered.

Policeman: I need you to take a breathalyser test.
Motorist: What's a breathalyser?
Policeman: It's a bag that tells you how much you've drunk.
Motorist: I've got one of those at home.

Psychiatrist: Nurse, when someone asks if we're busy, just say yes. Don't keep saying, 'It's a madhouse here.'

What should you do with dead radiographers?

Barium.

Roger: I'm a self-medicating kleptomaniac.

Bert: What do you mean'?

Roger: When it gets bad I take something for it.

What does a bee use to brush his hair?

A honeycomb.

Why are fishmongers mean?

Because their job makes them selfish.

Son: Dad, why didn't God make Eve first?

Dad: He didn't want anyone telling him how to make Adam...

What do you call a nun on the run?

A roaming Catholic.

Did you hear about the idiot who got an AM radio for Christmas?

He gave it away because he said he only listened to the radio in the afternoon.

Employee: I'd like a £5 per week pay rise, please.
Boss: I was thinking more of doubling your hours and halving your holiday.
Employee: Don't be ridiculous!
Boss: Well, you started it.

Boss: Jones, at your interview, you said you had five years' experience and now I find this is your first job.

> **How do you measure laryngitis?**
>
> In hoarse-power.

Jones: Yes, but you said you were looking for a candidate with imagination.

Diner: Waiter, there are no strawberries in my strawberry cheesecake.
Waiter: Well, there's no angels in the angel cake either.

Why is bullfighting a safe profession?
There's only one danger, and even that is
avoid-a-bull.

**Why do alien spaceships have UFO written
on them?**
Because they run on Unleaded Fuel Only.

**What do you get if
you cross a parrot,
an umbrella and
a goat?**

Polyunsaturated
butter!

**Son: Did Dad surprise you when he ordered
in French at the restaurant last night?**
Mum: He certainly did – it was an Indian restaurant.

Careers officer: Now, when you're looking for a job, remember that hard work never hurt anyone.
Pupil: That's the trouble – I'm really looking for something with an element of danger.

Which are the healthiest bees?

The vitamin bees.

If a shrewd Scotsman disappears into thin air, is he canny or uncanny?

First man: I wish I hadn't cleaned the garage with my wife today.
Second man: Why's that?
First man: I can't get the cobwebs out of her hair.

What happened when the billy goat and the nanny goat fell out?
They decided to stay together for the sake of the kids.

An Englishman, a Frenchman, a Turk, an Iraqi, an Indian, a Korean, an Australian, a Peruvian and a Mexican decided to visit a posh restaurant. The doorman stopped them on the way in and said, 'I'm sorry, gentlemen, but you can't come in here without a Thai.'

Son: Mum, why does the Queen have to do her own housework?
Mum: I'm sure she doesn't.
Son: But I heard them say on the telly that last night she swept down the staircase before meeting her guests.

Son: Mum, do we get vegetable oil from vegetables and sunflower oil from sunflowers?
Mum: Yes, son, that's right.
Son: So where do we get baby oil from?

A man in the street had an anorak tied to a piece of string and the anorak was somehow jumping all around the place, like it was alive. Passers-by watched in amazement and threw money into the anorak, which the man collected.

Eventually a policeman came by and said, 'I'm going to have to confiscate that.'

'But you can't take it away,' protested the man, 'that's my livelihood.'

First skeleton: Hadn't you used to be a mummy?

Second skeleton: Yes, but I went on holiday to unwind.

Geography teacher: Where is Felixtowe?

Jimmy: On the end of Felix' foot.

The teacher was trying to get her class to think on their feet. 'Sally, how would you complete the saying if it started, "If at first you *do* succeed..."?' '... try not to look surprised,' suggested Sally.

Why did the catgut leave town without telling anyone?
It wanted to get out of the tennis racket.

Horace was visiting Herbert and happened to look in the fridge.

'Why have you got an empty milk bottle in here?' he asked.

'In case anyone wants a black coffee,' replied Herbert.

Son: Mum, I think Dad's a bit depressed.
Mum: What makes you say that?
Son: He's got the Samaritans on speed-dial on his phone.

How do we know Robinson Crusoe was efficient?

He had all his work done by Friday!

What do you get if you cross a pitbull with a collie?
A dog that bites your leg off then goes to fetch help.

Prosecutor: Did *you* kill the victim?

Witness: No.

Prosecutor: Do you know the penalty for perjury?

Witness: I know it's less than the penalty for murder.

Customer: Can I have the whole salmon from the window, please, and can you throw it to me.

Fishmonger: Why do you want me to throw it to you?

Customer: Because I've been fishing all day and I want to be able to tell my wife I caught it.

Man: Tell me, darling, do you like rings?

Woman: Oh, yes!

Man: Good, I've entered you for the boxing tournament on Saturday.

Music teacher: Don't forget to lock the piano when you've finished, Jane.

Jane: But all the keys are on the inside, miss.

Teacher: Which is more important, the sun or the moon?
Pupil: The moon, miss.
Teacher: Why do you say that?
Pupil: Well, the moon gives light at night when we need it, but the sun only shines during the daytime when we don't.

Diner: What goes best with a jacket potato?
Waiter: I'd recommend the button mushrooms and Thai noodles.

An idiot decided to start a chicken farm, so he bought a hundred chickens from another farmer. After a week he was back to buy another hundred chickens. A week later he was back again for more.
'You must be doing well,' said the farmer.
'Not really,' said the idiot, 'in fact all my chickens keep dying. I think I'm planting them too deep.'

First man at funeral: Twenty clowns at that circus, and poor Buttons was the most popular – I can't believe they've only sent one car of mourners.

Second man: Ah, but just wait and see how many get out of it.

Son: I'm confused by the weather forecast.

Dad: Why?

Son: Well, the weatherman said it'll be zero degrees today and twice as cold tomorrow.

What do you call a gunfighter who drinks nothing but lemonade?

Wyatt Burp.

Son: You know you said the back of my legs under my knees were calves?

Mum: That's right.

Son: Well, when I grow up will they be cows?

Jimmy: I'm a bit worried about tomorrow.

Johnny: Just go to sleep, it's Christmas Eve.

Jimmy: Yes, but Dad just dashed outside and I heard him shout, 'I don't care who you are, fatso, get those reindeer off my roof!'

Teacher: Ronald, I've taught you everything I know, and you're still ignorant.

Ronald: I know, sir. Are you sure you're in the right job?

How do you buy bargain chickens?

Offer the farmer a poultry sum.

Mum: Where are you going with the cat and that pair of scissors?

Son: Dad said we'd got a bit of money in the kitty and I'm just going to find out how much.

Railway inspector: What would you do if you realised two trains were heading towards each other on the same line?

Signalman: I'd change the points to divert one of them.

Inspector: And if the points were broken?

Signalman: I'd shut both signals to red.

Inspector: And if the signals failed?

Signalman: I'd flag them down with my shirt.

Inspector: And if it was at night?

Signalman: I'd flag them down with my lamp.

Inspector: And if your lamp was out of batteries?

Signalman: I'd go and fetch my brother, Charlie.

Inspector: Why would you fetch your brother?

Signalman: Well, he's never seen a train crash before.

First woman: Is that a mink stole your husband's given you?

Second woman: Well, I'm not sure it's mink, but I think it's probably stole.

What's invisible and unpopular?

A fart in a lift.

Charlie: Why did you give up your job at the medicine factory?
Eric: It was too quiet for me – you could hear a cough drop.

Bert: I was planting some seeds in the middle of the High Street the other day, and what do you suppose came up?
Derek: I don't know.
Bert: A policeman.

How does a lawyer get to sleep?
First he lies on one side, then he lies on the other.

Patient: Doctor, I keep thinking I'm turning into a small bucket.
Doctor: Yes, you do look a little pale.

What's yellow and white
and travels at 100mph?

A train driver's egg sandwich.

Why did the King Edward and the Jersey
Royal hate John Motson.

He's a common tater.

A couple were woken in the middle of the night
by a knocking at their door. The man opened
a window and asked what was the matter.

'Can you give me a push?' asked the stranger.

The man was just about to refuse when his wife
said, 'John, don't you remember last year when
we broke down and someone helped us? Now
it's your turn.'

'I'll be out in a minute,' he called down.

After putting on some clothes and shoes,
John went down and opened the door but
no one was there.

'I'm over here,' called the stranger, 'on the swings!'

Mum: Where shall we go on holiday next year?

Son: I'd like to go somewhere I've never been before.

Mum: How about the bathroom?

The trainee lumberjack was summoned to his boss's office. 'How come you're only cutting down ten trees a day?' he demanded.

'I don't know, boss, but I missed my training, I was ill.'

Hearing this, the boss calms down and takes him outside. 'OK, let's go through it again – give me your chainsaw.'

The trainee hands it over and the boss starts it up.

'Whoa,' says the trainee, 'what's that noise?!'

What's yellow and flashes?

A banana with a loose connection.

Customer: Have you any invisible ink?

Assistant: Certainly sir, what colour?

> **What's black and white, flies and lives under the sea?**
>
> A puffin in a submarine.

The teacher thought he'd try some reverse psychology on his pupils. 'Everyone who thinks they're stupid, stand up,' he asked.

No one moved, but eventually Jim rose slowly from the back of the class.

'Do you think you're stupid, Jim?' asked the teacher.

'Not really, sir, I just hate to see you standing there on your own.'

A man was getting nothing done at work, as his workstation was cluttered with figurines – Marilyn Monroe, Che Guevara, Mao Tse-Tung, Gandhi, James Dean, etc. A colleague walked past and said, 'You've got an IT problem.'

'What do you mean?' asked the man.

'You've got too many icons on your desktop.'

What did the interrogator say to the pig?
We have ways of making you pork.

Why do demons and ghouls stick together?

Because demons are a ghoul's best friends.

Teacher: Can anyone define what a circle is?
Herbert: It's a round straight line with a hole in the middle.

Teacher: Can anyone name a creature that was half-man, half-beast?
Toby: Buffalo Bill, miss.

First zombie: Have you met my girlfriend?
Second zombie: Good grief! Where did you dig her up from?

What do you get if you cross a yeti and a vampire?

Frostbite.

A man turned up at a bed and breakfast very late one night. He rang the doorbell and the lady opened the bedroom window and peered out.

'What do you want?' she snapped.

'I'd like to stay here, please,' asked the man.

'Well, stay there then!' she said, slamming the window shut.

Diner: Waiter, this vinegar's very lumpy.

Waiter: Those are the pickled onions, sir.

**Patient: Doctor,
I think I've got Dutch flu.**

Doctor: What do you mean?

Patient: Well, I'm all clogged up.

What goes 'Buzz, zzub, buzz, zzub ...'?

A bee glued to a yo-yo.

What does it say
at the top of an
idiot's ladder?
Stop.

Teacher: Who broke this window?
George: It was Tommy. I threw a brick at him and
he ducked.

Son: Dad, can I have 50p if I'm good today?
Dad: Why can't you be more like me? I'm good
for nothing.

**A man was walking through the Olympic Village
when he saw an athlete carrying a long stick.
He went up to him and asked, 'Are you a
pole vaulter?'**
The athlete replied, 'No, I'm German. But how did
you know my name?'

Billy: Mum, you know that family vase that's been handed down from generation to generation?

Mum: Yes.

Billy: Well, this generation's dropped it.

Passenger: Captain, this sailor just insulted me, he said I was fat.

Captain: Is this true, sailor?

Sailor: All I said was, 'Avast behind!'

A man staggered home the worse for wear with a duck under his arm.

'Don't you bring that pig in here,' said his wife.

'In case you hadn't noticed,' said her husband, 'it's a duck.'

'I was talking to the duck.'

The gap between how old a Dad imagines himself and how old his kids see him as is exactly 17 years and 3 months.

DAD STAT

Fortune teller: Your husband is going to be murdered.

Woman: Was I acquitted?

What should you do if a gorilla runs in your front door?

Run out the back door.

Jimmy: I've got loads of damned homework to do tonight.

Mum: Don't use words like that in this house.

Jimmy: But William Shakespeare says it.

Mum: Well, you're not to play with him any more.

Auntie: Anyone who can guess what I've got in my hand can have a kiss.

Jimmy: An elephant!

Auntie: Close enough, come here!

Deep sea diver: I am about to begin my ascent now, over.

Ship's radio: Don't bother to come up, we're sinking.

Teacher: Jimmy! Why are you scratching yourself?

Jimmy: Because no one else knows where I itch, miss

What happened to the singer who put on a show for a tribe of cannibals?

He went down really well!

Doctor: I've got some bad news and some good news. The bad news is we had to amputate your legs.

Patient: And what's the good news?

Doctor: The man in the next bed wants to buy your slippers.

Where do birds drink coffee?

In a nest-café.

What happened when Lee decided to eat nothing but garlic for a week?

He became Lone Lee.

Dad's To Do List
(and Why It Never Gets Done)

1. Tidy the Garage (It's really not worth doing until all the kids have left home)

2. Wash the Car (I did it last year and it just got dirty again)

3. Mow the Lawn (Mother Nature will take care of it in Winter)

4. Clean the Windows (The ladders are at the back of the garage – see job 1)

5. Change the Spent Light Bulbs (It'll save energy if I wait until they've all blown)

6. Clean out the Hoover (but it's a hoover – how can it possibly need cleaning!)

7. Pick up Tom from football practice (The walk home will strengthen his leg muscles)

8. Walk the Dog (It gets enough exercise from disobeying me)

9. Take stuff to the recycling centre (Put it on eBay and let people come to us)

10. Bring in the shopping from the car (Let's just get a takeaway)

Grandad: I bet I can do something you can't do.
Jimmy: What's that?
Grandad: I can sing and brush my teeth at the same time.

What did the book reviewer say about the world's heaviest book?
'I couldn't pick it up.'

Who is the world's worst gentlemen's entertainer?
Jack the Stripper.

What did the boy woodworm say to the girl woodworm?
What are you doing in a joint like this?

What happened to the man who was arrested for stealing milk, vanilla essence and cornflour?
He was remanded in custardy.

Dad: None of the matches in this box will light!
Son: That's strange, because I tested them all yesterday.

Horace: I've just been to Grease.
Herbert: Where's your suntan, then?

Colin: Do you think I could be accepted at medical school, sir?
Teacher: Possibly, after you're dead.

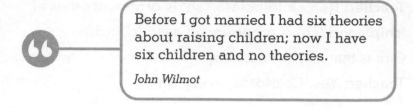

> Before I got married I had six theories about raising children; now I have six children and no theories.
>
> *John Wilmot*

What's the difference between a useless boxer and a nail?

One gets knocked out and the other gets knocked in.

Teacher: Can anyone think of a job where you need a torch?

Ronnie: A burglar, miss.

Diner: Could I have a bag to take the leftovers for our dog, please.

Diner's son: Great, we're getting a dog!

Teacher: Today we are looking at antonyms. What is the opposite of woe?

Dennis: Giddy-up!

Teacher: Remember class, 'sh' is pronounced as in 'ship', and 'ch' is pronounced as in 'church'
Girl: Is that every time, miss?
Teacher: Yes, Charlotte, every time.

> **Where did the butterfly couple meet?**
>
> At the moth ball.

> **What do you call a useless, incontinent ostrich?**
>
> A dire rhea.

Teacher: Clive, put that chewing gum in the bin.
Clive: I can't do that, miss, my brother only lent it me for this morning.

What happened to the angry vampire?
He flipped his lid.

Son: Thanks for lending me that money, Dad. I shall forever be in your debt.
Dad: That's what I'm afraid of.

What's grey and furry on the inside and white on the outside.
A mouse sandwich.

Teacher: What am I going to do about your work and behaviour, Walter?
Walter: Well, Mum says if you think I'm stupid and lazy you should see my Dad.

Son: Dad, what does coup de grace mean?
Dad: I think it's French for lawnmower.

Who stole Little Bo-Peep's sheep?
The shepherd's crook.

First teacher: The standards of maths in this school are appalling.
Second teacher: I know! Half my class don't know their times tables, half of them can't add up, and the other half can't even count!

Teacher: Sally, what are the five continents.

Sally: Er, a, e, i, o, u.

Mum: You got the job, then?
Dad: Yes, they said they gave it me because they couldn't find anyone better.

What do you get
if you cross a
Labrador with
a snail?
A pet that will go to
the shops and bring you last week's newspaper.

Music teacher: I wish you were playing on the
radio, Jimmy.
Jimmy: Do you think I'm that good, miss?
Teacher: No, but at least then I could switch
you off.

What guards Buckingham Palace and has 100 legs?
A sentrypede.

Mum: Our kids do brighten up the home,
don't they?
Dad: Well, they certainly never turn any flippin'
lights off.

Herbert: What makes you think your brother's mean?

Horace: Well, last month he found a crutch and broke his leg just so he could use it.

Sally: Dad, the boys at school say my legs are like matchsticks.

Dad: Well, they're wrong – your legs don't match at all.

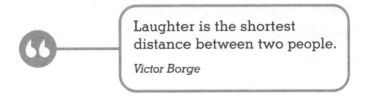

Laughter is the shortest distance between two people.

Victor Borge

Sherlock Holmes and Dr Watson returned home one night to find themselves locked out of their flat.

Watson went off to find Mrs Hudson but when he returned Holmes had already let himself in with a key he'd fashioned from a piece of fruit.

'How on earth did you do it, Holmes?' he asked.

'Lemon entry, my dear Watson.'

> **What grows between your nose and your chin?**
>
> Tu-lips!

Motorist: Could you tell me how to get to Lower Widdle, please.
Yokel: Lower Widdle … I don't think you can get there from here.

Theatre director: I've just auditioned your wife for Oedipus the King.
Friend: Jocasta?
Director: No, she was terrible.

Interviewer: I'll give you the job if you can answer this question: which bird doesn't build its own nest?
Herbert: The cuckoo.
Interviewer: Well done, you'd be surprised how many people don't know.
Herbert: It was easy – everyone knows cuckoos live inside clocks.

Teacher: Can anyone give me an example of how heat expands and cold contracts?

Tommy: Well, the days are longer in summer and shorter in winter, miss.

Horace: Why have you got a hand grenade tied to each ear?

Herbert: You know that idiot who comes in every night and bangs me round the ears? Well tonight I'm going to blow his hands off.

Son: Mum, which month do you think Dad drinks the least beer?
Mum: February.

What's a cannibal's favourite meal?

Snake and pygmy pie.

Someone's just invented a pencil for idiots.
It's got a rubber at both ends.

Why was the uninhibited librarian sacked?
She had no shelf-control.

What sort of bandage do you wear after open-heart surgery?
Ticker tape!

First caterpillar: Have you made any New Year Resolutions?
Second caterpillar: Yes, I'm turning over a new leaf.

What do you call a dyslexic vegetarian highwayman?
Kid Turnip.

Why do penguins carry fish in their beaks?
Because they haven't got any pockets.

Grandson: Thanks for the socks, Gran, but why have you given me three?
Gran: Your mum said on the phone you'd grown another foot since the last time I saw you.

Teacher: This homework doesn't look like your handwriting, Tommy.
Tommy: No, miss, I borrowed my Dad's pen.

44% of Dads think it's time for flares to make a comeback, while the other 56% didn't realise they'd gone out of fashion in the first place.

DAD STAT

Maths teacher: How do you divide 10 potatoes equally between 6 people?
Billy: Mash them, sir.

Teacher: Jimmy, what is Britain's highest award for valour?
Jimmy: Nelson's Column.

> **How did the football fan burn his ear?**
>
> He was listening to the match.

What actor do you get if you cross a Christmas tree with a river?
Douglas Firbanks.

Two carpenters were working in a house. One said, 'Why are you throwing away all those nails?'
'The heads are on the wrong end.'
'You idiot – we can use them on the opposite wall.'

How do you stop a
dog barking in the
back of your car?
Put him in the front.

What do you get if
you cross an elk with
an Easter egg?
Chocolate moose.

Teacher: Mrs Giles, I know your little boy is from
a farming family, but could you ask him to stop
going on about it in class? It's all 'manure' this
and 'manure' that.
Mrs Giles: Do you know how long it's taken us to get
him to only say 'manure'?

What do you call the ghost of a policeman who
haunts hotels?
The inn-spectre.

Doctor: I haven't seen you for a while, Mr Smith.
Patient: No, I've been ill.

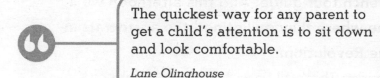

The quickest way for any parent to get a child's attention is to sit down and look comfortable.

Lane Olinghouse

Pupil: How old are you, miss?

Teacher: How old do you think I am?

Pupil: About twenty-five?

Teacher: I'm flattered, what makes you say that?

Pupil: I counted the rings around your eyes.

Son: Dad, there's a man at the door collecting for the old folks' home.

Dad: Tell him to hang on while I go and get your gran.

Customer: Why do these painkillers have superglue in the ingredients?

Chemist: They're for splitting headaches, sir.

French tour guide: And this afternoon we'll see where they guillotined the aristocrats in the Revolution.

Tourist: That's all I need, another visit to a chopping centre.

Horace: Did you hear a giraffe and a snake have escaped from the zoo?

Herbert: Yes, they're searching high and low for them.

Jimmy: What did you win that medal for, Grandad?

Grandad: It was awarded me by mistake in the North African campaign. I was on patrol in the desert and I sent back a coded message – 'Rommel captured' – and they gave me the medal.

Jimmy: What was the mistake?

Grandad: I meant to say 'Camel ruptured'.

How do you catch fish with maracas?

Cast a net.

What is the most common lie in the world?

'I have read and agree with the licence conditions.'

A little boy was sitting by the side of a drain in the road with a fishing rod. A little old lady went past and decided to humour him.

'How many have you caught?' she asked.

'You're the sixth,' he replied.

How do you make a pear drop?

Let go of it.

Man: Someone's just stolen all my teacups.

Policeman: Ah, you've been mugged then.

Dad: How did the shed window get broken?

Son: I was cleaning my catapult and I didn't realise it was loaded.

Mum: What's this bucket of horse manure doing in the living room?!
Dad: You told me to get the flies out of the kitchen.

> **What happened to the idiot who sat on the floor?**
>
> He fell off.

Mum: Are you sure you've had driving lessons?
Dad: Yes, I took a crash course.
Mum: That explains it.

What did the idiot do when he found a creepy-crawly in his ear?
He shot it.

Diner: I don't like all these flies in here.
Waiter: Well, point out those you do like and I'll chase the rest out.

Herbert was watching a long funeral procession go past when Horace came up to him.

'Who's dead?' asked Horace.

'I'm not sure,' replied Herbert, 'but I think it's the chap in the first car.'

Who runs the chip shop in the Arabian Desert?

Sultan Vinegar.

Woman: I'd like a fur coat, please.
Assistant: Certainly, madam, what fur?
Woman: To keep warm, of course.

Herbert and Horace were walking home from the pub when they met two nuns walking arm-in-arm going the other way. When they reached the men the nuns split up and went either side, before linking up again.

'Blimey, Horace,' said Herbert, looking behind him, 'how on earth did she do that?'

Tourist: Why is the town hall flag at half-mast?
Mayor: We're half-expecting the Queen.

What happened when two athletes were cremated at the same time?
It was a dead heat.

Psychiatrist: I think I've cured your son's gambling problem. Today he bet me £50 I had a false beard, so I got him to tug it as hard as he could and then he had to pay me. That'll teach him.
Dad: No it won't. He bet me £100 this morning you'd ask him to pull your beard at his next appointment.

Why does Julius's girlfriend like Friday nights?

Because that's when Julius Caesar.

Jimmy: Can Charlie come out to play?

Mum: Sorry, he's got to do his homework.

Jimmy: Well, can his football come out to play?

Why did the team of DVD players win all its football matches?

Because they had fast forwards.

What happened to the man who drank a bottle of Harpic?

He went clean round the bend.

What do you call an owl wearing a toupee?

Hedwig.

Diner: Waiter, this water is cloudy.

Waiter: No it isn't, sir, we just haven't cleaned the glass.

What do you call a fawn who keeps surprising people?

Bamboo.

Teacher: Your shoes are worn out, Billy
Billy: I've got some new ones, miss, but I'm leaving them off until I've got used to them.

What starts with 'e', ends with 'e' and only has one letter?
An envelope.

Teacher: Bobby, I thought you were going to do farmyard impressions, but I can't hear anything.
Bobby: Just wait a few seconds, miss – I'm not doing the sounds, I'm doing the smells.

What's the difference between a sailor and a soldier?
Have you ever tried dipping a sailor into your egg?

Dad: There's a salesman at the door with a funny face.

Mum: Tell him you've already got one.

Man: I've come about the job as handyman.

Boss: And are you handy?

Man: I'll say! I only live next door.

Visitor: Is Farmer Giles in?

Mrs Giles: You'll find him in the pigsty. He'll be the one wearing a hat.

Teacher: What did Marconi invent?

Billy: Pasta, miss?

Does a gymnast prefer salt or pepper on his food?

It depends: in winter pepper, but in summer salt.

The teacher sneezed and his false teeth flew out of his mouth and smashed on the floor. 'It'll take me weeks to get another pair,' he moaned.

'Don't worry, sir,' said Tommy. 'My dad can get you a new set for tomorrow.'

Sure enough, the next day Tommy brings in a pair of false teeth and they fit perfectly.

'Your dad must be a wonderful dentist, Tommy,' says the teacher.

'Oh, he's not a dentist – he's an undertaker.'

Polly: My boyfriend's given me this beautiful pure wool jumper.

Patsy: But the label says 'cotton'.

Polly: I know, but he said that was only there to fool the moths.

Horace: My sister's having a baby.

Herbert: Does she know if it's going to be a boy or a girl?

Horace: I think it'll be one or the other, yes.

> **Why couldn't the medical student lance the patient's boil?**
>
> He kept falling off his horse.

First student: I can't work out if my dad's mean or stupid.

Second student: Why?

First student: Well, he's just sent me a letter that ends, 'I was going to send you a tenner, but had already sealed the envelope'.

Mum: I'm fed up with your mother staying with us – she'll have to go!

Dad: *My* mother? I thought that old lady was *your* mother.

Why don't teachers look out of the window in the morning?

Because then they'd have nothing to do in the afternoon.

Robber: OK, this is a stick-up! Hand over all the money!

Bank clerk: This is your first time, isn't it?

Robber: What makes you say that?

Bank clerk: You've sawn the wrong end off your shotgun.

Parent: I see Ofsted have said the school stands 'at the edge of a precipice'.

Head: Yes, but I intend to take us forward immediately.

Mum: Your dad's gone without his lunch again, run and pop this on the bus, Jimmy.

Jimmy: Which bus, Mum?

Mum: Any of them, he works at the Lost Property Office.

Herbert: Does your sister know whether she's expecting a boy or a girl yet?

Horace: No, I still don't know whether I'm going to be an aunt or an uncle.

Guard: Can you move your suitcase from that seat, madam?

Passenger: I'll have you know I'm one of the directors' wives.

Guard: I don't care if you're his only wife, you'll still have to shift it.

Policeman: Could you describe the man who assaulted you?
Herbert: That's what I was doing when he hit me.

Son: Why does Dad's face look like that?
Mum: Well, my theory is that when God was giving out noses your Dad thought he said 'roses' and asked for a big red one. Then when he was giving out chins he thought he said 'gins' and asked for a double.

Colonel: Well, sergeant, there's bad news and good news. The bad news is, we're surrounded, outnumbered, low on ammunition, and only have horse manure to eat.
Sergeant: What's the good news?
Colonel: We've got absolutely loads of horse manure.

How did the idiot crash his helicopter?

He was a bit cold so he turned the fan off.

What's pink and fluffy?

Pink fluff.

What's blue and fluffy?

Pink fluff holding it's breath.

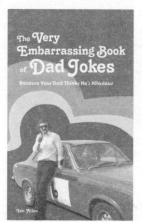

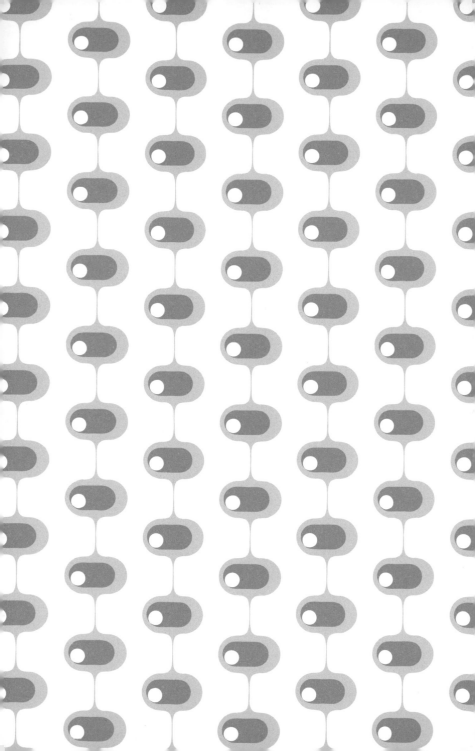